A TASTE OF
CUBA

LINETTE CREEN

A TASTE OF
CUBA

RECIPES FROM THE
CUBAN-AMERICAN COMMUNITY

A DUTTON BOOK

DUTTON

Published by the Penguin Group
Penguin Books USA Inc., 375 Hudson Street,
New York, New York 10014, U.S.A.
Penguin Books Ltd, 27 Wrights Lane,
London W8 5TZ, England
Penguin Books Australia Ltd, Ringwood,
Victoria, Australia
Penguin Books Canada Ltd, 2801 John Street,
Markham, Ontario, Canada L3R 1B4
Penguin Books (N.Z.) Ltd, 182-190 Wairau Road,
Auckland 10, New Zealand

Penguin Books Ltd, Registered Offices:
Harmondsworth, Middlesex, England

First published by Dutton, an imprint of New American Library,
a division of Penguin Books USA Inc.
Distributed in Canada by McClelland & Stewart Inc.

First Printing, June, 1991
10 9 8 7 6 5 4 3 2 1

REGISTERED TRADEMARK — MARCA REGISTRADA

LIBRARY OF CONGRESS CATALOGING IN PUBLICATION DATA:

Creen, Linette.
    A taste of Cuba : recipes from the Cuban-American community /
Linette Creen.
        p.   cm.
    Includes index.   18.95
    ISBN 0-525-24970-2
    1. Cookery, Cuban.   I. Title.
TX716.C8C74   1991
    641.597291—dc20   90-24648
                                                       CIP

641.597291
CRE

7/91

Printed in the United States of America
Set in Esprit

Designed by Steven N. Stathakis

ACKNOWLEDGMENTS

A very special thanks to my colleague, Anita Weil, a gifted writer whose cheery personality made working on this book together a pleasure. My deepest thanks to my family: my mother, Suzy Bloom, who let me be creative in the kitchen at an early (and messy) age; my stepfather, Gene, and my brother, Will; my dad, Bill Hoglund, and his wife, Jan, for their words of support; my sister, Laurie, and her husband, Brian, who are always willing to taste my recipes; my littlest brother, Jonathan; my favorite chef, Uncle Jeff; and my grandma Shirley. And thanks to the Creen family: Mr. and Mrs. Creen, Laura, Michael, Kenny, Mary, and Grandma, for their warmth and encouragement. Much appreciation to my agent, Faith Hornby Hamlin, who always pushes me in the right direction, and to our editors Molly Allen and Toni Rachiele, for their insightful guidance and excellent editing. And thanks to Cynthia Ventura of Ventura Translations and Mr. James Maguire for his enthusiasm and support.

I would also like to thank Marina Pina and her family for first introducing me to Cuban food. Much appreciation to José Barreiro of Cornell University for his information on the Taíno Indians. And for sharing their knowledge of the finer points of Cuban cooking, I'd like to thank Marcelino Hernandez, master chef of the Havana Clipper restaurant in Coconut Grove; Raoul Alfonso of La Carreta restaurant in Little Havana; Guillermo and Rebecca del Cristo, Mrs. Maria Carmen Myers, Jackie Hobales, and my good friend Barbie Rosen.

And finally, much love and gratitude to the most dedicated taste tester of these recipes (and also the ones that didn't make it into this book), my husband and love blossom, Joey Creen, Jr.

CONTENTS

FOREWORD, by Felipe Rojas-Lombardi   xi

INTRODUCTION   1

THE ELEMENTS OF CUBAN CUISINE   7

SPECIAL INGREDIENTS   15

APPETIZERS   29

SHRIMP IN GARLIC WINE SAUCE • SAUSAGE EMPANADAS WITH
PIMIENTO SALSA • PLANTAIN CROQUETTES WITH TOMATO-
CILANTRO VINAIGRETTE • SWEET RUM SHRIMP • ESCABECHE •
SPICY CRAB CAKES WITH PAPAYA CHUTNEY • PAPAYA CHUTNEY •
MAYONNAISE • FRIED SHRIMP WITH COCONUT-BEER BATTER AND
ORANGE COCKTAIL SAUCE • CONCH FRITTERS WITH CILANTRO
DIPPING SAUCE • FRUIT SALAD WITH LEMON-LIME DRESSING

SOUPS   47

FISH STOCK • CHICKEN STOCK • BEEF STOCK • SWEET PLAN-
TAIN SOUP • TRADITIONAL BLACK BEAN SOUP • CHILLED YUCA
SOUP • CREAM OF GARLIC SOUP WITH CILANTRO • GARLIC-
TOMATO SOUP • GALICIAN POTAGE • COLD CUCUMBER AND
AVOCADO SOUP • SHRIMP, CORN, AND POTATO SOUP • WHITE
BEAN AND TOMATO SOUP • CONCH CHOWDER • CHICKEN AND
RICE SOUP • RED BEAN SOUP • SWEET AND SPICY CALABAZA
SOUP • VEGETABLE SOUP WITH LENTILS AND RICE

FRUITS AND VEGETABLES   71

FRIED SWEET PLANTAINS · MASHED GREEN PLANTAINS ·
TOSTONES · YUCA WITH GARLIC SAUCE · CALABAZA FRITTERS ·
BONIATO CHIPS · BONIATO DUMPLINGS · RUM-GLAZED
BONIATOS · AJIACO · FRESH CORN AND RED PEPPER TAMALES ·
PEPPERS STUFFED WITH SPANISH SAUSAGE, RICE, AND TOMATO ·
VEGETABLE AND CHEESE OMELET · AVOCADOS WITH VINAIGRETTE

RICE AND BEANS   91

LONG-GRAIN WHITE RICE · BLACK BEANS · BLACK BEANS AND
RICE · YELLOW RICE · YELLOW RICE AND PEAS · RUM-
FLAVORED BLACK BEANS AND RICE · MARINATED BLACK BEAN
SALAD · SPICY BLACK BEANS WITH TOMATOES, ONIONS, AND
PEPPERS · RED BEANS AND RICE · SWEET BAKED WHITE BEANS
AND PORK · TRI-COLORED BEAN SALAD WITH BACON DRESSING ·
CHILLED LENTIL SALAD WITH SPICY VINAIGRETTE · HONEY-RUM-
BAKED BLACK BEANS · BLACK BEAN FLAN · BLACK BEAN
CHILI · MOLD OF YELLOW RICE WITH SHRIMP, SCALLOPS, AND RED
PEPPER

BEEF   115

ROPA VIEJA · ACHIOTE OIL · PICADILLO · OXTAIL STEW ·
PALOMILLA STEAK · BAKED YUCA STUFFED WITH SHREDDED BEEF
· CUBAN POT ROAST · TAMALE PIE WITH SWEET AND SPICY MEAT
FILLING · SPICY STUFFED PEPPERS WITH TOMATO SAUCE · MEAT-
AND-ONION-STUFFED TURNOVERS · PASTELES · FLANK STEAK
WITH PORT WINE MARINADE · ROLLED STUFFED STEAK

PORK   137

BRAISED LOIN OF PORK WITH PAPAYA · PORK TENDERLOIN
SAUTÉED WITH BITTER ORANGE AND GARLIC · BABY BACK RIBS
WITH SPICY PAPAYA SAUCE · HOMEMADE SPANISH SAUSAGE ·
CIDER-AND-MANGO-ROASTED HAM · ROAST PORK WITH PEPPERED
BLACK BEAN SAUCE · SPICY HAM AND POTATO CROQUETTES ·
PORK TAMALES · PORK CHOPS IN WINE SAUCE · FRIED PORK AND

ONION PATTIES • GRILLED GARLIC PORK • CORNMEAL-AND-RAISIN-STUFFED PORK CHOPS • HOT PEPPER PORK CHOPS WITH CREAMY GRAVY • SWEET AND SOUR PAPAYA PORK • CUBAN-CHINESE ROAST LOIN OF PORK

POULTRY   159

CHICKEN AND RICE • CHICKEN AND RICE STEW • BREAST OF CHICKEN AL AJILLO • SPICY CHICKEN SAUTÉ WITH VEGETABLES AND PAPAYA • COCONUT-STUFFED CHICKEN BREASTS WITH LIGHT CREAM SAUCE • COUNTRY BAKED CHICKEN • CHICKEN CROQUETTES WITH SAUTÉED ONIONS AND PEPPERS • ROASTED CHICKEN WITH PAPAYA GLAZE • ROASTED GAME HENS WITH BITTER ORANGE GLAZE • SWEET AND SPICY CILANTRO CHICKEN • GOLDEN BAKED CHICKEN WITH TOMATOES, OLIVES, AND CAPERS • CRISPY FRIED MARINATED CHICKEN • GARLIC-MARINATED ROASTED CHICKEN • PASTEL DE MAÍZ • SOFRITO GRILLED CHICKEN • SOFRITO SAUCE

SEAFOOD   187

PAN-FRIED GROUPER WITH ALMONDS • SALT COD, ISLAND STYLE • BAKED SALT COD • BLACK-BEAN-STEAMED SNAPPER • TUNA STEAK WITH SWEET RED PEPPER SAUCE • SNAPPER IN COCONUT SAUCE • LOBSTER AND RED PEPPERS IN A RICE MOLD • BROILED DOLPHIN WITH SWEET RED PEPPER AND PAPAYA CHUTNEY • SHRIMP CREOLE • MARINATED CONCH SALAD • SEAFOOD STEW • BREADED SHRIMP WITH TOMATO-CAPER SALSA • SNAPPER WITH SAFFRON SAUCE • POMPANO WITH SHRIMP SAUCE • SPICY GRILLED TUNA • SNAPPER GRILLED IN FOIL WITH CILANTRO, TOMATO, AND ONION • POACHED POMPANO WITH ORANGE-RUM SAUCE • SHRIMP WITH BLACK BEAN SAUCE

BREAD   213

CASSAVA BREAD • CUBAN BREAD • TOMATO-PIMIENTO BREAD • CHEESE BREAD • CASSAVA ROLLS • SWEET PLANTAIN BREAD • PAPAYA AND RAISIN BREAD • ALMOND-RAISIN BREAD •

ORANGE BREAD • SPICY CORNBREAD WITH GREEN CHILIES • CHURROS • SWEET CORNBREAD • CORNMEAL BREAD • COCONUT MUFFINS • SPICY RED PEPPER MUFFINS • GARLIC-ONION DINNER MUFFINS • MANGO BUTTER

DESSERTS   237

DIPLOMATIC PUDDING • TRADITIONAL FLAN • COCONUT-RUM FLAN • COUNTRY-BAKED ALMOND FLAN • PLANTAIN CUSTARD • FROZEN RUM MOUSSE • BAKED RUM-RAISIN PUDDING • CLASSIC RICE PUDDING • OLD-FASHIONED CORNMEAL PUDDING • BACON FROM HEAVEN • FRIED YUCA DOUGH WITH ALMOND SYRUP • ALMOND COOKIES • FRESH COCONUT AND BANANA CREAM PIE • SPONGE CAKES WITH RUM • VANILLA BEAN ICE CREAM • FLAMING MANGO SAUCE OVER HOMEMADE VANILLA ICE CREAM • FROZEN BANANA CUSTARD • COCONUT ICE CREAM • MANGO ICE CREAM • PINEAPPLE ICE CREAM • GUAVA ICE CREAM

BEVERAGES   265

CUBAN COFFEE • CUBAN COFFEE WITH MILK • ICED CUBAN COFFEE • HOT CHOCOLATE COFFEE • RUM-SPIKED COFFEE • PAPAYA-BANANA BATIDO • GUAVA BATIDO • PAPAYA-MANGO BATIDO • SPICED CALYPSO PUNCH • COCONUT MILK • COCONUT WATER • CUBA LIBRE • PRESIDENTE • MOJITO • RUM COCKTAIL • CUBAN COCKTAIL • CUBAN SPECIAL • RUM SWIZZLE • SUPER RUM SWIZZLE • LIME DAIQUIRI • MANGO DAIQUIRI • PEACH DAIQUIRI • PINEAPPLE DAIQUIRI • BANANA DAIQUIRI • PIÑA COLADA • YELLOW BIRD • RUM AND COCONUT WATER • COLD RUM TODDY • HOT RUM TODDY • RUM PUNCH • PLANTER'S PUNCH • MILK PUNCH • SANGRÍA

A HOLIDAY FEAST   299

ROAST SUCKLING PIG • ROASTED BONIATOS • ROASTED SWEET ONIONS • ORANGE-RAISIN CORNMEAL STUFFING • SAUTÉED BUTTER-RUM PLANTAINS • PAELLA • RUM RICE PUDDING

INDEX   311

FOREWORD

It was not such a long time ago that my appetite for Cuban food was awakened. In fact, it was not until I met my good friend Cuban-born Maricel Precilla, a Ph.D. in Spanish History, a food historian, but above all an excellent cook. It was in my kitchen that she shared with me a variety of native dishes such as tostones, which became a staple in my restaurant, The Ballroom.

It is hard to ignore the exquisite chicken and rice dishes, called arroz con pollo, that the Cubans master so beautifully, or the magnificent conch chowder, the richly textured sweet plantain soup, or the yuca with garlic sauce. What would a traditional dinner be without Moros y Cristianos, which is a satisfying combination of perfectly flavored black beans served along with plainly cooked rice, flavored with a hint of garlic. Cuban cooking is accentuated by the generous use of fresh garlic, cilantro, and aromatic spices, such as annato, also called achiote.

The recipes collected in Ms. Creen's book are as mouth-watering as their preparation is easy. *A Taste of Cuba* is a delicious representation of the personality of Cuban food.

— FELIPE ROJAS-LOMBARDI

INTRODUCTION

I will never forget my first Cuban dinner. It was 1977 and I had recently moved to a Cuban-American neighborhood in Miami Springs. In school I met a girl named Marina Pina, who invited me to have dinner at her house. Marina's grandmother prepared the meal: a savory *ropa vieja*, hearty black beans and rice, sweet fried plantains, and a delectable flan for dessert. For the Pina family, this was an ordinary dinner, but for me it was a revelation. I fell in love with Cuban cooking and decided to learn all I could about it.

With the warmth and hospitality that I found to be typical of Cuban-Americans, Marina's mother and grandmother welcomed me into their kitchen. There, and in the households of other friends, I learned how to prepare the traditional dishes that Cubans have enjoyed for centuries.

After school, my girlfriends and I would often drive to Calle Ocho (S.W. 8th Street), the main street of Miami's Little Havana section. We'd treat ourselves to refreshing *batidos* (fruit milkshakes) and *churros* (fried dough with sugar) from outdoor stands. At the informal cafetins, we'd snack on *tostones* (fried green plantains), *croquetas* (croquettes), and *pasteles* (spiced meat patties). Frequently, I'd strike up a conversation with the person behind the counter, practicing my Spanish and learning how to prepare these tasty snacks.

When I was asked out to dinner, I'd suggest that we eat at one of the Cuban restaurants in Little Havana, Miami Springs, or Hialeah. At these restaurants I tasted many of the soups, appetizers, desserts, and seafood, pork, and beef entrées you'll find in this book.

During my Miami years, I had the good fortune to participate in many Cuban celebrations, which always include plenty of good eating. For most Cuban-Americans, Christmas is the most important holiday of the year. One December, my neighbors invited me to help prepare and partake of a traditional Cuban Christmas Eve dinner. As we worked in the kitchen, the grandmother, who was supervising the cooking, reminisced about the Christmases on her family farm in the Camaguey province. On the morning of Christmas Eve, they would slaughter a pig they had raised and then begin cooking. Other families would arrive from neighboring farms, and there would be singing and dancing to the music of Spanish guitars. On this Christmas in Miami, we ate the same foods the grandmother had had as a child sixty years ago: roast suckling pig, paella, boniatos (Cuban sweet potatoes), plantains, Moros y Cristianos (black beans and white rice), and flan. The holiday feast that concludes this book is based on this memorable meal.

Pork is the traditional fiesta food that Cubans serve on special occasions: weddings, birthdays, christenings, and Festival de los Tres Reyes (Festival of the Three Kings, also called Epiphany). Festival de los Tres Reyes, which is celebrated in January, is almost like a second Christmas. Santa Claus brings the children gifts, sweets, and fruit, and families gather for feasting.

Another festive time of the year is Carnival. Cuban Carnival differs from the Brazilian version in that it is not held before Lent; in Havana and Santiago de Cuba, Carnival is in July, and in Miami it is in mid-March. Cuban Carnival has its roots in Santería, which was originally the religion of the Cuban slaves, and mingles Catholicism and African tribalism. Once a year, the cabildos (secret societies of Santería) would parade down the streets in fanciful costumes, performing comparsas (street dances) to the rhythm of African drumming. This event grew into Carnival, a time of the year when rich and poor, young and old alike, would adorn themselves with feathers, sequins, and masks and gather for weekends of wild revelry.

Miami now hosts a ten-day Carnival featuring special performances and a colorful parade down Calle Ocho; vendors selling foamy beer, shots of rum, batidos, and Cuban snacks; and musicians playing famous Latin rhythms such as the mambo, the cha-cha, and the rumba.

I had another chance to hear this intoxicating music at the quince parties I attended. Quinces, which celebrate a girl's fifteenth birthday and her coming of age, are a Cuban tradition, and wealthy families in Miami host spectacular affairs.

My first quince was astonishing, although I found out later that it was typical of these events. The quinceanera wore a white hoop-skirted ballgown and sat on a lace-covered throne, attended by her tuxedoed escort and the gowned girls of her Honor Court. There were toasts with champagne and sparkling cider, and an incredible amount of food: a towering pyramid of tropical fruit salad, mounds of shrimp and conch salad, a large roast suckling pig, *picadillo* (Cuban-style beef hash), *arroz con pollo* (chicken and rice), baked grouper and red snapper, rice and beans, yuca, plantains, and more. For dessert, there were several types of flan and ice cream, pastries, and a four-tier cake with a miniature quinceanera on top. I tasted many of the recipes in this book for the first time at quince parties, where I spent a lot of time talking to the older women about the food. My friends teased me because I was more interested in discussing recipes than dancing.

As you can imagine, it was hard to leave all the fun and festivities in Miami—not to mention the weather. But after high school my family moved to Alaska, where I ran a seafood store and wrote my first cookbook. In that cold climate, I missed Miami terribly, especially the warmth of my Cuban-American friends and their families.

When I relocated to New York City, I was pleased to find that the ingredients of many Cuban dishes were available in Hispanic markets and there were a number of Cuban and Chinese-Cuban restaurants to visit. I also found excellent Hispanic markets and restaurants in the Union City/West New York area in New Jersey, which has the second largest population of Cuban-Americans in the country.

Still, I missed the unique Cuban ambience of Miami, where approximately 600,000 Cuban-Americans reside. Whenever possible, I would return to Florida to visit old friends and try new restaurants. In recent years, I noticed a trend: "nouvelle" Cuban restaurants, where the chefs use traditional ingredients in creative new ways. In this book, you will find adaptations of some of the memorable dishes I had in these modern Cuban restaurants, as well as the classics.

I would like to thank the chefs and restaurateurs who took the time to share their talents with me; the experts who taught me about the history of Cuban cuisine, and, most of all, my Cuban-American friends and their families, who taught me to cook the way they had been taught in their grandmothers' kitchens.

Cuban cooking has, until now, remained mostly an oral tradition, passed down from chef to apprentice, from mother to daughter. By writing this cookbook, I hope to help preserve this culinary heritage and also explore the diversity of Cuban food. Whether you are a Cuban-American yourself or have had your interest sparked by partaking of Cuban food, I'm sure you will enjoy the exciting flavors of Cuban cuisine.

THE ELEMENTS OF CUBAN CUISINE

In general, the ingredients in Cuban dishes are not very expensive and the cooking techniques are not too complicated. This is down-to-earth, family food. In the Cuban culinary tradition, there is no strict delineation between haute cuisine and peasant fare. In Cuba, wealthy people ate meat more frequently than did the poor, many of whom subsisted largely on rice, beans, root vegetables, and plantains. The well-to-do had a more varied diet than the poor and often had cooks who were skilled at seasoning; however, the basics were similar among all the classes.

This is a cuisine of meat lovers: pork and beef dishes are favored, and chicken is served frequently, usually paired with rice. Since Cuba is surrounded by the sea, there are also many enticing fish and seafood dishes. Although tomatoes, onions, garlic, peppers, and lively seasonings spice up the entrées, they are generally mild rather than hot. Mild green chili peppers (chilies) are usually used instead of red hot chilies, so the food of Cuba is not as fiery as that found in other Hispanic countries. Cuban dishes are often sweet as well as spicy. Sugarcane has been Cuba's largest crop for centuries, and sugar is added to many entrées and side dishes.

Green vegetables and green salads rarely appear on Cuban tables; starchy side dishes are preferred (however, salads are occasionally made to accompany a meal). Fried plantains, boniatos, yuca, and rice and beans are typical accompaniments at lunch and dinner. Plantains and yuca are Cuba's most versatile foods and are used to make everything from appetizers to desserts. Beans are also a staple and are often cooked into hearty soups served with Cuban bread, a light, airy type of loaf, as well as rice.

Cuban desserts are luxurious: very sweet and often creamy. Flans (caramel custards), puddings, and tropical fruit-flavored ice creams are among the favorites. For liquid refreshment, there are tropical fruit milkshakes, called *batidos*, and many more potent rum concoctions from the days when Havana was known as the cocktail capital of the world.

Cuban food reflects the Cuban spirit: a hearty appetite for enjoying the sweetness and richness of life, and a respect for tradition coupled with adventurousness. The food also reveals the history of Cuba and the diverse groups of people who have inhabited the island.

Cuban cuisine is a melting pot of ingredients and cooking techniques from around the world. These international elements include: Cuba's native fruits and vegetables; the agricultural and cooking techniques of the Taíno Indians; the culinary traditions of Spain and Portugal; the livestock and crops introduced by the Spaniards; the contributions of the African slaves and Chinese laborers; and the foods of other Spanish colonies.

THE EVOLUTION OF CUBAN COOKING

It was the Taíno-Arawak Indians of Cuba, a peaceful people with a highly developed agriculture, who are believed to have introduced Columbus, and thereby Europe, to both tobacco and corn, or maize, which gets its name from the Taíno word *mahiz*. The Taínos boiled and roasted corn and made it into flour.

The Taínos also cultivated boniato (Cuban sweet potato), calabaza (Cuban pumpkin), malanga (a root vegetable), chili peppers (chilies), and yuca (also called cassava). Yuca, a root vegetable that was their most important crop, was so essential to the Indians that they had various religious rites centered on it. The Taínos made it into cassava bread, a flat bread cooked on a griddle, which the Spaniards later took on their long sea voyages, since it could be dried and stored for up to two years. The Taíno Indians also included yuca in ajiaco, a vegetable soup/stew that was the mainstay of their diet. The Spaniards added pork and beef to this ancient recipe.

Since Cuba is an island with over two thousand miles of coastline, seafood has always been an important part of the Cuban diet. The Taíno Indians developed fisheries and fish corrals to gather the tuna, red snapper, grouper, shrimp, and other species found in Cuba's warm Gulf Stream waters. They cooked these fish by grilling them over an open fire on a grating of thin green sticks, which was called a *barbacoa*, the prototype of today's barbecue.

Cuba is blessed with a varied terrain: mountains, rivers and streams, fertile valleys, and rolling plains. The island is so lush that when Columbus first landed, he thought he had found the original Garden of Eden.

The Taíno Indians also introduced the Spaniards to Cuba's edible fruits, which include avocados, papayas, coconuts, pineapples, and guavas. Sadly, their hospitality was repaid with brutal exploitation by the Spanish conquistadors. The Taíno civilization was destroyed except for small groups of survivors who escaped to the mountain regions. But the culinary legacy of this gentle tribe continued to give sustenance to Cuba's new inhabitants.

The Spaniards introduced to Spain the produce they found in Cuba and the other lands they explored, most notably Mexico. These gifts from the New World revolutionized Spanish cooking. Many of the foods we think of as being typically Spanish include ingredients that the conquistadors brought back from their travels — most notably, peppers and tomatoes.

It was a reciprocal exchange between the Old World and the New World, however, for while the Spaniards used many of the fishing and agricultural methods that the Taíno Indians had developed and ate foods that were native to the island, they also planted major new crops, including beans, rice, citrus fruits, mangos, coffee, and sugarcane.

Slaves were brought in from Africa to work the large plantations that the Spaniards established. On the plantations, the slaves did most of the cooking in kitchen buildings that were separate from the planters' great houses. The slaves' diet consisted largely of black beans and rice, yuca, boniatos, and plantains, and they developed imaginative ways to season and prepare such staples, which the planters and their families ate as side dishes with fish and meat.

Early on in their settlement the Spaniards brought livestock to Cuba: horses, cattle, chickens, and pigs. Vegetables and seasonings that were native to the island were added to Spanish meat dishes. For example, *ropa vieja*, Cuba's famous shredded beef, was originally Spanish, but in Cuba peppers and achiote oil were added. Achiote oil is made with annatto seeds, which have an orange-red color and were used by the Indians to decorate their bodies. Achiote oil is also used to flavor *picadillo*, a spicy chopped beef hash that is descended from an old Moorish dish; the Cuban version added tomatoes and peppers.

Cuban cuisine also developed a Portuguese flavor, because many of the island's settlers came from the areas of Spain near Portugal. They brought with them a love of seafood dishes and salt cod, which the Portuguese imported from Newfoundland. The rich garlic- and tomato-flavored soups that Cubans prepare are typically Portuguese, as is the heavy use of parsley, cilantro, long-grain rice, and sweet peppers. The intriguingly named almond cake called Bacon from Heaven, a popular Cuban dessert, originated in Portugal.

Dishes were also imported to Cuba from Spain's other colonies. Pasteles arrived from Puerto Rico; tamales and enchiladas came from Mexico.

Another element was added to Cuban cuisine in the mid-nineteenth century, when plantation owners became worried about numerous slave uprisings and sought an alternate source of labor. Between 1853 and 1873, more than 132,000 Chinese workers were brought to Cuba under eight-year contracts to do agricultural, domestic, and commercial work. After working through their contracts, many Chinese people established their own businesses, including numerous Chinese restaurants in Havana.

Today, there are many Chinese-Cuban restaurants in the New York/New Jersey area and in Miami. These restaurants generally serve both typically Spanish and typically Chinese dishes, although there is some mingling of Oriental spices and Cuban ingredients. A few Cuban dishes have stir-fried vegetables and Oriental seasonings; however, the Chinese taste for green vegetables was never fully assimilated into Cuban cuisine.

THE HEYDAY OF CUBAN CUISINE

When sugarcane prices soared after World War I, resulting in what was called the "dance of millions," scores of hotels, restaurants, mansions, and casinos were built in and around Havana. During the next four decades, vacationers flocked to Cuba for the beautiful beaches, the casinos, and the exciting nightlife. Havana became the playground of the world.

Bacardi's popular light rum, which was developed in Cuba in the nineteenth century, was mixed into inventive cocktails by Havana's creative bartenders. Fresh fruit Daiquiris, Cuba Libres, Mojitos, and Presidentes were served up in the well-known bars such as the Floridita and in nightclubs such as the Tropicana, which was renowned for its spectacular floor show.

Many of the restaurants catering to foreigners served continental cuisine, while others introduced people from around the globe to Cuban specialties. Palomilla steaks, oxtail stew, shrimp *al ajillo* (in garlic wine sauce), and paella were some of the Cuban dishes tourists especially enjoyed.

There were many fine restaurants on the island, but perhaps the best meals were served in the homes of the upper- and middle-class Cubans, who often had talented cooks. The general eating pattern was to start with a light breakfast of bread, *café con leche* (coffee with milk), and fruit juice, followed by a mid-morning break for coffee and sweet snacks. Luncheons were substantial: Soup was often served, then an entrée of meat, fish, or fowl, accompanied by rice and beans, plantains, yuca, or another vegetable, and a rich dessert to cap off the meal. In the evening, it was customary for families to dress for dinner and enjoy hearty repasts that included appetizers, soup, entrées, several side dishes, and desserts.

CUBANS IN AMERICA

This way of life came to an end after the revolution led by Fidel Castro in 1959. Hundreds of thousands of Cubans left their beloved island, and most of them settled in the United States. There are now over a million Cuban exiles in this country. Sadly, in Cuba, food rationing is in effect and there are recurrent food shortages, but in America, Cuban cuisine is flourishing.

Cuban-American families tend to be close-knit, and the Cuban custom of enjoying good food with loved ones and friends is being carried on in this country. I hope the recipes in this book will help you share in this pleasure.

SPECIAL INGREDIENTS

Most of the ingredients used in the recipes in this book can be found in supermarkets or grocery stores. In recipes where unusual ingredients are used, I suggest where they might be purchased. In most cases, this will be in Hispanic markets (also called Spanish or Latin markets), which have sprung up in the many areas of the country where there are Hispanic communities. If you have difficulty locating a Hispanic market, gourmet shops or the gourmet section of your grocery store are other sources of exotic items.

Cuban cooking generally uses basic cooking techniques. Where necessary, instructions on cooking techniques and handling specific ingredients are given in chapter and recipe introductions. In this chapter, you will find advice on handling some of the more frequently used ingredients that can be a little tricky.

BEANS

Black Beans. Black beans, or *frijoles negros*, a staple in Cuban cooking, are the type of beans most commonly used in Cuban cooking. They can be purchased dried in most food markets. Dried beans need to be picked through and cleaned before using. Sift through them with your hand to eliminate any particles of gravel or dirt, then place in a colander and rinse them well under cold water.

It is best if you can soak dried beans in fresh water for 8 to 10 hours at room temperature before cooking them. However, if you do not have time to soak the beans, you can add 1 hour to the cooking time.

To soak dried beans: Begin by boiling the beans in a large pot in water to cover for 2 to 5 minutes. Then allow them to stand in the water at room temperature for 8 to 10 hours (or overnight, if that is more convenient). A good way to test if the beans have soaked sufficiently is to break a bean in half lengthwise. If the color is the same along the outer rim as on the inside, they are ready to be cooked.

Lentils. Lentils are eaten around the world and are the oldest type of bean known. They need to be cleaned and rinsed in the same manner as black beans, but they do not require soaking. Their cooking time is shorter than that of other beans, only about 20 minutes. Watch closely, because they can soften easily and lose their texture and shape.

Red Beans. Red beans, which are also known as kidney beans, can be found dried in most food markets. They need to be cleaned, rinsed, and soaked in the same manner as black beans.

White Kidney Beans. White kidney beans can be purchased dried in most food markets. They should be cleaned, rinsed, and soaked in the same manner as black beans.

BITTER ORANGES

Bitter oranges, which are also known as Seville oranges, sour oranges, or *naranja agria*, are small fruit with flesh that is darker than that of navel oranges. Fresh bitter oranges are sold in Hispanic markets in Florida but are difficult to find in other parts of the country. However, bottled bitter orange juice is sold in most Hispanic markets, and this can be used in the recipes in this book.

BONIATOS

Boniatos are Cuban sweet potatoes, which are sold in Hispanic markets. They look similar on the outside to American sweet potatoes, and American sweet potatoes can be substituted if necessary, but they have white flesh instead of yellow. They also have a stronger, more bitter taste. When purchasing boniatos, check that they are rock-hard and have no mold or soft spots. Store them at room temperature. Always scrub them thoroughly before using.

CALABAZA

Calabaza, or Cuban squash, has orange skin and flesh. Although calabaza can be as small as melons, they are usually quite large, and are often sold halved or in large slices in Hispanic markets. When purchasing a whole calabaza, check that the rind has no soft spots or cracks and that a stem is attached. When buying cut calabaza, look for flesh that is close-grained, not dry or watery.

Whole calabaza can be stored for up to a month in a cool spot. Cut calabaza can be wrapped in plastic and stored in the refrigerator for a week.

To cut a whole calabaza, use a large sharp knife or cleaver. If you have difficulty, cut off the stem end, then place your knife lengthwise across the calabaza and use a mallet to carefully pound the blade (where it meets the handle) until it penetrates the rind. Once the calabaza is cut, scoop out and discard the seeds, then remove the meat with a paring knife.

CAPERS

You can buy Spanish capers, which are slightly larger than other varieties, in most supermarkets. When removing capers from a jar, use a small spoon rather than your fingers to prevent them from turning rancid.

CASSAVA. See YUCA.

CHILIES. See PEPPERS.

CHORIZO

Chorizo, or Spanish sausage, is spicy. The paprika, pepper, and other seasonings that are added to the sausage give it a bright red color and a pungent flavor. It can be purchased from some supermarkets or butchers, or you can make it yourself (see recipe on page 144).

CILANTRO

Many Cuban dishes are garnished or flavored with cilantro, an aromatic herb that is also called Chinese parsley or fresh coriander. It resembles parsley but has a stronger taste. Bunches of cilantro are sold in Hispanic markets, Oriental stores, produce stands, and many supermarkets. It can be refrigerated for about a week in a plastic bag, but do not wash it or remove the stems until you are ready to use it.

COCONUTS

Green coconuts (so called because of their green color, unlike that of the brown ones in our supermarkets) are immature coconuts. They are available in Caribbean, Hispanic, and specialty produce stores. They contain an almost clear liquid, called coconut water, and their meat is soft and moist and can be scooped out with a spoon. These young coconuts are the best type to use in fruit salads, or when you want fresh coconut water or coconut milk (see recipes on pages 279 and 278).

The meat of mature coconuts dries out and you can't hear much liquid sloshing around if you shake them. Mature coconuts are the best type to use when you need grated coconut.

Be sure to check the "eyes" of the coconut (three dark spots on one end). They should be smooth and dark; if they are wet or moldy, the coconut may be spoiled.

To open a coconut, use a small hammer and a clean nail to puncture two of the eyes. Drain the liquid into a bowl. With a hammer, give the shell a hard blow to split it. This blow should cause the shell to fall away from the coconut meat. Cut off any remaining meat with a paring knife.

Before grating a coconut, peel off the brown outer skin. Break the meat into small pieces and grate it with a hand grater. An average-size coconut (1 to 2 pounds) will yield 2 to 3 cups of grated meat.

CONCH

In many parts of the United States, fresh conch is unavailable but frozen conch meat is often sold in fish stores. Where fresh conch is obtainable, it is almost always sold cleaned. If not you can usually request that the fishmonger remove the conch meat from the shell and clean it for you.

If you wish to remove the meat and clean the conch yourself, use the claw of a hammer to make a hole in the shell 1 inch down from the crown, as near as possible to where the coil ends. Insert a knife into the hole and sever the muscle where it adheres to the shell. Once this muscle has been severed, you can easily remove the conch meat from the shell with a knife.

To clean the conch, use a knife to remove the intestines, and discard them. Peel off and discard the tough outer skin. Use a wooden mallet to pound the conch meat until it is tender but not torn. Cut the conch into pieces as the recipe specifies.

CORIANDER. See CILANTRO.

CORN HUSKS

Corn husks are used to make wrappings for traditional enchiladas and tamales. In summertime, you can purchase fresh corn, remove the outer leaves, and use the soft inner layer of husks. When fresh corn husks are unavailable, dried husks can be purchased in Hispanic markets. These husks need to be reconstituted with water before using.

To reconstitute corn husks, place the husks in a small bowl of hot water and let sit 30 minutes till soft and pliable.

CORNMEAL

Cornmeal comes in many colors, including white and blue, but yellow is the type most commonly used in Cuban cooking. Yellow cornmeal is available in most grocery stores.

CRABS

Some crabs have gills that are toxic, so I recommend asking your fishmonger to clean them for you. You may also choose to buy prepicked crabmeat, which is sold in many fish stores. If you do, be sure that you are buying real crabmeat, not imitation crabmeat made from other fish.

If you choose to clean and pick the crab yourself, as with such crabs as the blue crab or Dungeness, begin by lifting the little tab that runs under the crab's stomach. Pull the tab until it starts to pull off the top shell, and use your hand to completely remove the shell. Discard the top shell unless you wish to use it in soup stock.

In the stomach cavity, you will see spongy, off-white gills on both sides. Remove the gills and all the body organs in the center of the crab and discard. Rinse the crab well under cold water.

On both sides of the crab's body, you'll see white meat divided by three pieces of cartilage into small sections. Using a seafood cracker or lightly using a hammer, crack the shell. Pick the meat out of the crevices.

FISH

Most of the fish recipes in this book call for either shellfish or fish fillets. When buying fish fillets, check that the texture of the flesh is firm and elastic. There should be very little smell; an overly pungent fishy odor or iodine smell indicates that the fish is not fresh.

Although fillets are usually sold skinned and boned, it is a good idea to check them for small bones that may not have been removed. Rub your fingers over the fillet to feel for bones, which usually run in a small line. Using a very small or pin-nose pliers, pull the bones out and discard them.

If your fish needs to be skinned, use a fillet knife or a small boning knife. Place the fish skin side down and run the blade between the skin and the flesh while holding one end of the fish down.

GARLIC

To prepare fresh minced or pressed garlic, break off as many garlic cloves as specified in the recipe. With a small paring knife, cut off both tips of each clove. Peel off the dry skin and discard it. Use a garlic press or mince the clove by hand with a chef's or chopping knife.

GUAVA

Guavas are sold in Hispanic markets and fruit stands. You can purchase them when they are yellow and tender or buy them slightly green and let them ripen at room temperature. Ripe guavas should be used within two days. They can be refrigerated for a day or two.

LENTILS. See BEANS.

MALANGA

Malanga is a Cuban root vegetable with patchy, thin brown skin and beige or pinkish flesh. Malanga are shaped like long yams and can weigh from ½ pound to over 2 pounds. When purchasing malanga in a Hispanic market, look for tubers that are very hard, with juicy, crisp flesh. Malanga should be stored at room temperature and peeled before boiling.

MANGOS

There are many varieties of mangos, ranging in size and color. The type most commonly found in Hispanic markets and fruit stands in the United States is green, and kidney-shaped, and weighs about half a pound. Green mangos are unripe and should be placed on a sunny windowsill to ripen.

When they turn pink or yellow with brown or black spots, they are ripe and ready to use.

IMPORTANT NOTE: Mangos secrete a fluid that can cause an allergic reaction in some people. For this reason, it is suggested that you wear rubber gloves when peeling mangos and wash your hands carefully afterward.

Mangos peel easily, but their juicy flesh tends to cling to the pit.

To cut a mango into chunks, use a very sharp paring knife. Lay the mango on its flattest side, cut a slice off the top, then turn it over and cut off another slice. Cut these slices into chunks, then cut the remaining flesh off the pit.

ONIONS

Onions should always have the dry outer skin peeled off and discarded. When using a whole onion for flavoring, use a paring knife to slice ⅛ inch off the top, then peel off the dry outer skin. Cut off only the dead fibers at the end of the root, then lightly score an X on the root.

To slice an onion, cut it lengthwise from the top to the root end. Place it cut side down and slice crosswise. To chop or mince it, begin by cutting lengthwise from the top to the root end. Place the onion cut side down and cut in vertical slices, then in horizontal slices. Continue chopping until the onion pieces are the desired size.

PAPAYAS

Papayas are sold in Hispanic markets and fruit stands, sometimes green and sometimes ripe. When green, they should be ripened on a windowsill until they turn orange and soften.

IMPORTANT NOTE: Papayas secrete an enzyme that can cause skin eruptions or swelling in allergic people. Therefore, it is advisable to wear rubber gloves when peeling papayas and to wash your hands thoroughly afterward.

PEPPERS

Cuban cooking is less "hot" in its degree of spiciness than the foods of many other Hispanic and Caribbean countries. Hot red chilies (chili peppers) are not used a great deal. Instead, you will find that red and green bell peppers are favored. These peppers are usually seeded and deribbed (the ribs inside the pepper are removed) before being added to the dishes.

In the recipes that include chilies in this book, I suggest using mild green chilies. (Canned green chilies come in mild, hot, and extra hot). These do not require handling with rubber gloves, as hot red chilies do, and are a great deal milder.

To roast peppers, preheat the oven to Broil. Cut the peppers in half lengthwise, then remove the ribs and seeds and discard them. Place the peppers on a cookie sheet lightly greased with olive oil. Broil them for 4 to 6 minutes until their skin blisters and blackens. Remove them from the oven and place them in a paper or plastic bag for 5 to 10 minutes. Remove the peppers from the bag and peel off the blackened skin (which should come off easily) before using.

Cayenne pepper, which is dried pre-ground hot red pepper (also called chili pepper), is added to some Cuban dishes. It is readily available, usually sold in small spice containers in grocery stores.

Whenever black pepper is called for, I recommend using whole black peppercorns, which you grind through a pepper mill before adding.

PLANTAINS

Plantains are widely available in Hispanic markets, fruit and vegetable stands, and many supermarkets. They vary in shape and size, and their color depends on their degree of ripeness. Unripe plantains are green and hard, with a starchy, vegetable-like taste. As plantains ripen, they turn yellow, then become mottled with dark spots. Ripe plantains, which are sweet and soft, are brownish-black color, resembling overripe bananas. In the recipes in this book, the type of plantain that should be used will be specified. To ripen green plantains, keep them in a warm place until they turn yellow, then brownish-black.

Ripe plantains can be peeled easily, like bananas, but green plantains require a little more care, since their skin clings to the fruit. To peel a green plantain, use a sharp paring knife to cut off ¼ inch from each end. Make lengthwise slits along the folds in the skin (four slits per plantain), being careful not to cut the inside of the fruit. Pull the skin off one strip at a time, using the knife to separate it from the fruit.

RICE

Rice, along with black beans, is a staple of Cuban cooking and is served almost every day in most households. I recommend using long-grained unconverted white rice, which can be found in most food stores. White rice can be stored indefinitely on your kitchen shelf, provided that the container is airtight and no moisture enters it. Once the rice is cooked, you can store it in a sealed container in the refrigerator for up to 10 days.

To reheat cooked rice, add 2 tablespoons of water for every cup of rice. Fluff the rice with a fork as you heat it over low heat.

Some Cuban recipes call for yellow rice, which is white rice that gains its color from saffron, turmeric, or chicken stock (see recipe, page 99). In paella, Valencia rice is used. This is a Spanish rice that is very tender and plump.

SHRIMP

Shrimp are a favorite Cuban shellfish and are used in many recipes. They usually have a strong odor, but if they have an ammonia-like smell, they have turned rancid and should not be purchased. The shrimp should look plump, with meat that is firm to the touch and clear, not cloudy or white in color. Their tails should be bright orange or red, not black or brown. Their eggs (if any) should be bright, not dark or soft, and should burst when pinched between your fingers.

When a recipe calls for cooked, peeled, and deveined shrimp, buy the amount of shrimp called for in the recipe (2 pounds of raw shrimp in the shell, also known as green shrimp, will give you 1 pound cooked, shelled shrimp).

Peel the shrimp by holding the tail of the shrimp in one hand and grasping the legs on one side of the shrimp in the other hand. Pull the legs up and around the body of the shrimp so that the shell follows.

Using a small pointed knife, make a shallow cut lengthwise down the back of the shrimp and rinse out the sandy vein under cold running water.

To cook 1 pound of shrimp, bring 4 cups of water to a boil in a large pot, along with 1 tablespoon salt, 1 bay leaf, 1 clove garlic, and ½ small onion. Add the peeled and deveined shrimp and let simmer 4 to 5 minutes, just until the shrimp are pink and have lost their translucence. If you cook them so long that they curl tightly, they will be tough. Drain and chill until ready to use. The shrimp may also be shelled and deveined and then cooked with their shells for added flavor.

SIDE PORK

Side pork is bacon that has not been cured or smoked. It is also known as streak of lean or uncured bacon. Side pork is very inexpensive and can be purchased sliced in many butcher shops. If it comes with the tough outer skin still on it, make sure you trim this off before using.

TOMATOES

Tomatoes of various sizes are frequently used in Cuban cooking, and are often peeled and seeded before adding. To facilitate peeling, core tomato and make an X on the opposite side by scoring 2 inches across and ⅛ inch deep. Then plunge the tomato into boiling water for 20 seconds. Remove the tomato with a slotted spoon and plunge it into ice water to stop the cooking. The skin should peel off easily with a paring knife. Cut the tomato in half and scoop out the seeds with a small spoon.

YUCA

Yuca (also called cassava) is a root vegetable that is sold fresh and frozen in Hispanic markets. Fresh yuca has hard white flesh and brown skin covered with what looks like bark. When purchasing yuca, check that there are no hairline cracks or mold, and that the smell is fresh and clean. If no yuca can be found, potato may be substituted, although you will sacrifice flavor.

Yuca should be stored in a cool place outside the refrigerator. If you use a small piece of the yuca, you can peel the rest and store it in the refrigerator for one day, covered with cold water. You can also peel the yuca, cut it into chunks, wrap it, and freeze it. It will last in your freezer up to three months if it is wrapped airtight.

To peel a yuca, scrub it first, then cut it in half crosswise, using a sharp knife. Quarter each section lengthwise, then peel the outside skin with the knife. Rinse the peeled yuca before cooking it.

To obtain 1 cup of mashed yuca, peel and quarter 1 medium-size yuca (1 average yuca weighs approximately ½ pound). Place the yuca in a medium-size saucepan of lightly salted boiling water. Reduce the heat to low, cover, and simmer 30 minutes. Remove from the heat and drain the yuca through a strainer. Transfer the yuca to a medium-size mixing bowl and mash with a fork or a potato masher.

APPETIZERS

The Cuban culture is a sociable one, and many Cuban-Americans enjoy lingering over drinks and appetizers before dining. At Cuban wedding celebrations, quince parties, and other affairs, dazzling arrays of imaginative appetizers are presented to guests. Another social custom in Miami is the *coctel*, a pre-dinner cocktail party where tasty "finger foods" such as croquettes, empanadas, and fried shrimp are served.

If you would like to throw a cocktail party with a Cuban flavor, serve several of the recipes in this chapter, along with a variety of the rum drinks in the Beverages chapter and a selection of beers.

SHRIMP IN GARLIC WINE SAUCE
Gambas al Ajillo

Makes 6–8 servings

This garlic sauce is a classic Cuban way to prepare shrimp, which is one of the most popular and frequently served appetizers at Cuban restaurants and parties.

2 teaspoons butter
¼ cup olive oil
4 cloves garlic, minced
1¾ pounds raw shrimp, peeled
*   and deveined (page 27)*

¼ cup white wine
2 tablespoons fresh chopped
*   cilantro*

In a sauté pan, melt the butter with the oil over medium-high heat. Add the garlic and sauté 1 minute. Add the shrimp and cook 2 to 3 minutes. Add the wine and cook 2 minutes, stirring frequently. With a slotted spoon, transfer the shrimp to a warm serving platter. Sprinkle with cilantro and serve.

SAUSAGE EMPANADAS WITH PIMIENTO SALSA
Empanadas de Chorizo con Salsa de Pimientos Morrones

Makes 12 empanadas

These empanadas are made with spicy Spanish sausage, which is also called chorizo. Chorizo is often served as an appetizer, with Cuban bread, with slices of pork and cheese, or fried. You can prepare chorizo yourself by using the recipe for Homemade Spanish Sausage on page 144 or purchase it from a Hispanic market or at some butcher shops.

EMPANADAS:

1½ cups flour
½ teaspoon salt
1 tablespoon sugar
4 tablespoons butter
1 egg, slightly beaten
3 tablespoons white wine

Flour for dusting surface
½ pound chorizo or Spanish Sausage (page 144), cooked, drained, and crumbled
Vegetable oil for frying

PIMIENTO SALSA:

½ cup chopped, drained pimientoes
1 tablespoon chopped fresh cilantro

2 tablespoons olive oil
1 tablespoon cider vinegar
Salt and freshly ground black pepper to taste

Mix the flour, salt, and sugar together in a medium-size mixing bowl. Cut the butter into the mixture, using a pastry blender or a fork. Make a well in the center of the flour mixture, and place the egg and wine in the well. Stir the mixture until blended.

Divide the mixture into 12 portions. On a floured surface, roll out 1 portion of dough into a circle, ⅛ inch thick. Place 1 tablespoon of sausage in the center and fold the dough together into a square. Seal the edges with a damp fork, then set aside. Repeat with the remaining dough, making 12 empanadas.

Heat oil in a deep fryer (3 to 4 inches, but no more than halfway full) to 375°F. Cook the empanadas, 4 at a time, in the deep fryer until lightly browned, approximately 4 to 6 minutes. Remove and place on paper towels to drain. Repeat with the remaining empanadas. When all the empanadas are fried, place them on a large serving platter and keep warm in the oven while preparing the salsa (or prepare the salsa ahead of time).

In a small mixing bowl, combine the pimiento, cilantro, olive oil, cider vinegar, salt, and pepper. Mix well and place in a small serving dish.

Remove the empanadas from the oven, place the salsa in the center of the platter, and serve immediately.

PLANTAIN CROQUETTES WITH TOMATO-CILANTRO VINAIGRETTE
Croquetas de Plátano a la Vinagreta con Tomate y Cilantro

Makes 24 croquettes

This recipe takes more preparation time than most, but will produce a delicious appetizer that is given an unusual flavor by the green plantains, which are starchy rather than sweet. If you plan ahead, you can prepare the croquettes in advance and be ready to simply fry and serve them when your guests arrive.

2 tablespoons butter
3 tablespoons flour
2 cups chicken stock (page 52)
1½ cups mashed, cooked green
   plantains (page 76)

¼ cup minced fresh parsley
¼ teaspoon white pepper
2 eggs, beaten
2 cups fine bread crumbs
Vegetable oil for frying

TOMATO-CILANTRO VINAIGRETTE:
2 large ripe tomatoes, peeled,
   seeded, and chopped
¼ cup chopped fresh cilantro

2 tablespoons olive oil
2 teaspoons cider vinegar

In a saucepan over medium heat, melt the butter with the flour, stirring until well blended. Add the chicken stock and cook over low heat, whisking frequently until reduced by half.

Place the plantains, parsley, and pepper in a large mixing bowl. Add ¾ cup of the chicken stock mixture and blend together. Cover the bowl with plastic wrap and cool the mixture in the refrigerator for at least 2 hours.

Remove the plantain mixture from the refrigerator and shape it into 24 cylinders (2 to 3 inches each). Place the eggs in a small bowl and the bread crumbs in another bowl. Roll the croquettes in egg, then in bread crumbs, and place on a rack to dry for at least 1 hour.

Fill a deep fryer with 2 to 3 inches of vegetable oil and heat to 375°F. Fry the croquettes, a few at a time, for 3 to 5 minutes, until golden brown. (If a deep fryer is unavailable, fill a large skillet a third full with oil and heat over medium-high heat. Fry the croquettes 3 minutes on each side in the skillet, until golden brown.) Remove the croquettes from the oil with a slotted spoon and let drain on paper towels. Transfer to a large serving platter and keep warm in the oven while preparing the salsa (or prepare the salsa ahead of time).

In a small mixing bowl, mix together the tomatoes, cilantro, olive oil, and vinegar. Transfer the salsa to a small serving bowl.

Remove the croquettes from the oven, place the salsa in the center of the platter, and serve.

SWEET RUM SHRIMP
Camarones Dulces con Ron

Makes 4 servings

This delectable appetizer features the sweet taste of rum, which has been associated with the Caribbean since it was first distilled in Barbados in the seventeenth century. There are dozens of different types of rum, but all are produced from sugarcane, the islands' chief crop. Although light, dry rum is the traditional Cuban variety, for this recipe I recommend a dark, full-bodied rum such as Myers's.

*Vegetable or peanut oil for
  frying
1 cup flour
1 tablespoon salt
1 pound raw large shrimp, peeled
  and deveined (page 27)*

*¼ cup Mayonnaise (page 41)
3 teaspoons honey
1 tablespoon dark rum
Greens, parsley, or watercress
  for garnish*

Fill a deep fryer with 2 to 3 inches of vegetable or peanut oil, and heat to 350°F. (If you do not have a deep fryer, fill a large skillet a third full with oil and heat over medium-high heat.)

In a medium-size mixing bowl or pie plate, combine the flour and salt. Dredge the shrimp 1 at a time in the flour until thoroughly coated. Fry the shrimp a few at a time for approximately 2 to 3 minutes, until golden brown. (If using a skillet, fry the shrimp on each side for 2 to 3 minutes.) Remove the shrimp with a slotted spoon and let drain on paper towels. Repeat with the remaining shrimp.

While the shrimp are frying, place the mayonnaise, honey, and rum in a medium-size saucepan. Cook over medium heat, stirring well, until the rum sauce is warm. Remove from heat.

When all the shrimp are fried, add them to saucepan and toss until all are coated with rum sauce. Transfer to a strainer. Drain off excess sauce by shaking the strainer lightly over the sink.

Place the shrimp on a large, warm platter garnished with leafy greens, parsley, or watercress, and serve immediately.

ESCABECHE

Makes 8–10 servings

Before the advent of refrigeration, the pickling process was relied upon as a quick and simple way to preserve fish or fowl. The pickling tradition lingered in Cuba, where widespread refrigeration was late to arrive. Escabeche, which means "pickled" in Spanish, is still popular today as a light, refreshing appetizer or lunch dish.

2 cups water
½ cup malt or white wine vinegar
½ cup olive oil
1 bay leaf, crumbled
½ teaspoon cayenne pepper
1 tablespoon salt
10 black peppercorns
2 large carrots, cut into julienne
1½ cups green beans, cut into julienne

4 medium onions, peeled and cut crosswise, paper-thin
1 small red bell pepper, seeded, deribbed, and cut crosswise, very thin
2 pounds skinned, filleted fish (snapper, swordfish, tilefish, or scrod), cut into 1½-inch cubes

In a medium pot, bring the water, vinegar, ¼ cup olive oil, bay leaf, cayenne pepper, salt, and peppercorns to a boil over high heat. Add the carrots and cook until tender. Remove the carrots with a slotted spoon and place in ice water. Repeat with the green beans. Remove the vegetables and set aside, along with the onions and peppers, reserving the poaching liquid.

In a deep skillet, heat the remaining olive oil over medium heat. When the oil is hot, add the fish cubes (as many as the skillet can hold without overcrowding the pan), and brown on both sides. Remove the fish with a slotted spoon and place on paper towels to drain.

When all the fish is brown and drained, transfer to a large, deep serving platter. Pour the reserved poaching liquid and vegetable mixture over the top of the fish and let cool. Chill in the refrigerator. Serve chilled.

SPICY CRAB CAKES WITH PAPAYA CHUTNEY
Croquetas de Cangrejo con Condimento de Papaya

Makes 6 servings

These delightful crab cakes are given a special Cuban accent by the cilantro. The papaya chutney is a sweet complement to the spicy crab cakes. In Cuba, papaya is sometimes called "fruta bomba," because of its resemblance to a hand grenade. See page 24 before handling papaya. This papaya chutney is delicious on fruit-sweetened breads (see Bread chapter), too.

1 pound crabmeat (page 22)
1 egg, beaten
¼ cup Mayonnaise (page 41)
1 tablespoon minced fresh cilantro
A few dashes of Tabasco sauce
½ teaspoon dried ground cumin
½ cup fine bread crumbs
A sprinkle of fresh ground white pepper
1 cup cornmeal for dredging
2 tablespoons butter for sautéing
Papaya Chutney (page 41)

In a large mixing bowl, combine the crabmeat, egg, mayonnaise, cilantro, Tabasco sauce, cumin, bread crumbs, and pepper. Use your hands to mix the ingredients together thoroughly, then form the mixture into small, round cakes, no more than ½ inch thick. Press each cake into the cornmeal so that each side is lightly coated.

In a sauté pan, melt the butter over medium heat. Sauté the cakes for approximately 5 minutes on each side, until golden brown. Drain on paper towels.

Place the crab cakes on a large platter and serve immediately, with Papaya Chutney alongside in a bowl.

PAPAYA CHUTNEY
Condimento de Papaya

Makes 6 servings

2 cups peeled, seeded, and diced
   papaya (page 24)
1 medium onion, peeled and
   diced
1 large red bell pepper, seeded,
   deribbed, and finely chopped
½ cup sugar

1 teaspoon ground ginger
½ teaspoon ground allspice
½ cup malt or cider vinegar
½ teaspoon salt
Dash of Tabasco sauce
1 cup water

In a large pot, combine all the ingredients. Simmer for ½ hour over low heat. Remove the chutney from the heat and allow to cool slightly before using.

MAYONNAISE

Makes 1½ cups

2 egg yolks
½ teaspoon salt
1 teaspoon prepared mustard

1¼ cups light olive oil or
   safflower oil
2 tablespoons white wine vinegar, or to taste

Make sure all your ingredients are at room temperature before you begin. In a medium-size mixing bowl, whisk together the egg yolks, salt, and mustard until well blended and salt is dissolved. Slowly whisk in the oil, adding drop by drop with a fork until you start to see a lighter color and the mayonnaise starts to thicken. Continue to add the oil in a slow, steady stream, whisking constantly, until all is blended together. Add the vinegar, a little at a time, to taste, and then use in desired recipe.

FRIED SHRIMP WITH COCONUT-BEER BATTER AND ORANGE COCKTAIL SAUCE
Camarones Empanados Fritos con Salsa de Naranja

Makes 4 servings

The coconut in the batter and the orange juice in the cocktail sauce lend this appetizer a tropical flavor, and the cayenne pepper adds a Spanish touch. It is perfect for cocktail parties, since it goes well with Piña Coladas (page 292), rum and orange juice, or beer.

ORANGE COCKTAIL SAUCE:

1 cup ketchup
2 tablespoons horseradish
Juice from ½ fresh orange

Dash of Tabasco sauce or to taste

BEER-BATTERED SHRIMP:

3 eggs
1 tablespoon vegetable oil
1 cup beer
1 tablespoon salt
¼ teaspoon cayenne pepper
2 tablespoons chopped chives,
½ cup shredded coconut
2 cups flour

Vegetable oil for frying
1 pound large raw shrimp, peeled and deveined (pages 26–27)
1 whole lemon
A sprinkle of salt
Sprigs of fresh parsley or cilantro for garnish

ORANGE COCKTAIL SAUCE: Combine the sauce ingredients in a small serving bowl and refrigerate until ready to serve.

BEER-BATTERED SHRIMP: Crack the eggs and separate, putting the whites into a small mixing bowl and the yolks into a large mixing bowl. Refrigerate the whites. Add the vegetable oil, beer, salt, cayenne pepper, chives, and coconut to the egg yolks. Gradually stir in the flour. Remove the egg whites from the refrigerator and whip until stiff. Carefully fold the egg whites into the batter.

Fill a deep fryer with 2 to 3 inches of vegetable oil and heat the oil to 375°F. (If you don't have a deep fryer, fill a skillet a third full with oil and heat over medium-high heat.)

Pat the shrimp dry with paper towels and dip into the batter, covering completely. Let excess batter drip off. Place 6 to 8 shrimp in the deep fryer and cook about 2 minutes, until golden brown. Remove with a slotted spoon and place on paper towels. Repeat the procedure with the remaining shrimp. (If using a skillet, cook the shrimp 2 to 3 minutes on each side, then remove with a slotted spoon and drain on paper towels.)

Cut the lemon in half and squeeze the juice over the shrimp. Lightly sprinkle the shrimp with salt. Arrange the shrimp on a warm serving platter and garnish with sprigs of parsley or cilantro. Remove the orange cocktail sauce from the refrigerator, place on the platter, and serve.

CONCH FRITTERS WITH CILANTRO DIPPING SAUCE
Frituras de Cobo con Salsa de Cilantro

Makes 4 servings

The conch, with its beautiful rose-tinted shell, symbolizes the Florida Keys, where many Cuban immigrants settled as early as the nineteenth century. Key West is nicknamed "Conchtown" and its year-round residents are called "conchs" or "konks." The white flesh of the conch is very popular in the Cuban community in Florida, where conch are found in abundance on the sea floor near the coastline. See page 21 for tips on handling conch. Orange Cocktail Sauce (page 42) is also good with these fritters.

CILANTRO DIPPING SAUCE:

¼ cup chopped fresh cilantro
½ teaspoon capers, chopped (optional)
1 cup mayonnaise

½ cup sour cream
¼ teaspoon lemon juice
Salt and freshly ground black pepper to taste

CONCH FRITTERS:

½ cup milk
1 package dry yeast
1 pound cleaned conch meat (page 21), chopped into ½-inch pieces
1 small onion, quartered
1 small green bell pepper, seeded, deribbed, and quartered

¼ cup chopped fresh parsley
¾ cup flour
1 egg
2 dashes of Tabasco sauce
½ teaspoon salt
Vegetable oil for frying
2 lemons, cut into wedges
Sprigs of parsley, cilantro, or watercress for garnish

In a small bowl, combine the cilantro, capers, mayonnaise, sour cream, and lemon juice. Add salt and pepper to taste. Place in the refrigerator to chill before serving.

In a small saucepan, warm the milk to 105° to 115°F.

Transfer the warm milk to a small ceramic dish and dissolve the yeast in it.

Place the conch, onion, and pepper into the workbowl of a food processor (with a steel blade) and process for 10 seconds. Add the milk and yeast mixture and the parsley, flour, egg, Tabasco sauce, and salt. Process for 1 minute, stopping when necessary to scrape the sides of the bowl. Cover the workbowl with a damp cloth, and let sit for 1 hour.

Place 2 to 3 inches of oil in a deep fryer and heat to 350°F. (or fill a large skillet a third full with oil and heat over medium-high heat). Carefully drop the batter by the teaspoonful into the hot oil, frying a few at a time, and deep-fry for 3 to 5 minutes. (If using a skillet, fry 4 minutes on each side.) Remove the fritters with a slotted spoon and place on paper towels to drain.

When all the fritters are fried and drained, transfer while still warm to a serving platter. Garnish with lemon wedges and sprigs of parsley, cilantro, or watercress. Remove the dipping sauce from the refrigerator and serve with the fritters immediately.

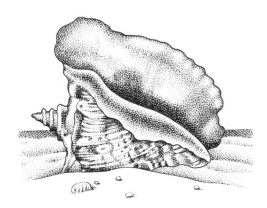

FRUIT SALAD WITH LEMON-LIME DRESSING
Ensalada de Frutas con Aliño de Lima-Limón

Makes 6 servings

Nothing is more evocative of the lush sensuality of island life than a colorful tropical fruit salad. This recipe contains my favorite combination of fruits, but almost any fresh seasonal selection can be used. Adding a splash of dark rum to this appetizer can turn it into a light dessert.

Fruit salad is particularly attractive when served in a large glass bowl which allows its colors to be seen. It also looks festive when served in watermelon or pineapple shells. Be sure to check page 24 before handling the papaya and mango.

1 papaya, peeled, seeded, and cut into 1-inch pieces (page 24)
2 bananas, peeled and sliced into bite-size pieces
1 mango, peeled and cut into 1-inch pieces (page 23)
1 cup pineapple, cut into 1-inch pieces

1 pint strawberries, washed, drained, and hulled
2 tablespoons fresh-squeezed lemon juice
2 tablespoons fresh-squeezed lime juice
2 tablespoons sugar
Handful of fresh mint leaves for garnish

Place all the fruit in a large salad bowl. Pour the lemon and lime juice over the fruit and sprinkle the sugar on top. Gently toss until all the ingredients are well combined. Garnish with mint leaves. Chill in the refrigerator, and serve cold.

SOUPS

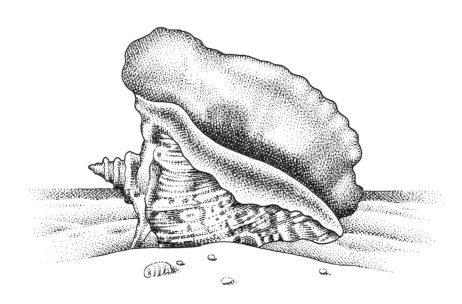

It might seem surprising that hot, thick soups are a specialty of a Cuban cuisine, considering the island's warm climate. But according to folk wisdom, food that is hot in temperature and seasoning is actually cooling and healthy, since it induces perspiration.

In many prerevolutionary Cuban households, it was customary for both lunch and dinner to begin with soup. Nowadays, many Cuban-Americans are too busy or calorie-conscious to eat heavily at lunchtime, but soup is still a popular way to begin a hearty dinner. These nutritious soups can also be satisfying lunches on their own, or accompanied by Cuban bread or white rice.

Traditionally, Cuban soups are very salty and peppery. You will notice, however, that in these recipes, I leave the amount of salt and pepper added to your discretion. Many people prefer to savor the more subtle flavors of a soup without heavy seasoning, while some like it hot. And those who are concerned about restricting their sodium intake for health reasons may choose to leave out the salt completely or use imitation salt.

Unless otherwise indicated, all of the following soups can be served immediately in pre-warmed bowls or tureens. They can also be covered and saved for up to one week in the refrigerator, and reheated before serving.

FISH STOCK
Caldo de Pescado

Makes about 8 cups

This stock is quick and easy to prepare. It offers a thrifty way to use the bones and heads that you trim from fish dinners. You can also purchase the trimmings directly from your fishmonger. Fish stock will last 2 to 3 days in the refrigerator and will keep up to 6 months in the freezer.

2 quarts water　　　　　　　　*2 sprigs parsley*
2 medium onions　　　　　　　*1 sprig fresh thyme*
2 carrots, peeled　　　　　　　*1 bay leaf*
1 celery stalk　　　　　　　　 *3 black peppercorns*
3 pounds fish trimmings, heads　*Salt to taste*
　and bones (no skin or gills)

Bring the water to a boil in a large soup or stock pot. Add all the ingredients, reduce the heat, and let simmer for 15 minutes.

Pour the stock through a strainer. (Do not press or squeeze the fish trimmings or the stock may become cloudy.) Discard the solids. Use the stock in another recipe, or refrigerate or freeze it for later use.

CHICKEN STOCK
Caldo de Pollo

Makes about 6 cups

Homemade chicken stock makes the most nourishing and flavorful base for soup, but it is time-consuming to prepare. In Cuban-American families, it is often the grandmothers who have the time at home to simmer the stock.

Chicken stock can be made the old-fashioned way, with two whole chicken carcasses from the butcher, or it can be made with two whole chicken breasts, skinless and with bones.

Make sure all excess fat has been trimmed off and discarded. It is also very important to skim the stock after it comes to a first boil, then to reduce heat and skim impurities often. Before using, skim off excess fat after straining by using a ladle or by letting the stock chill in the refrigerator and letting the fat rise to the surface and coagulate, then spooning off.

Stock can be saved in the refrigerator for up to a week, or frozen for later use. It's handy to freeze some of the stock in ice cube trays, so that when a recipe calls for a small amount it is easily accessible. Stock will keep up to 6 months frozen.

2 whole chicken carcasses
2 quarts water
2 large onions
4 whole garlic cloves
3 carrots
2 celery stalks

1 bouquet garni (made with 1 thyme sprig, 5 black peppercorns, and a parsley sprig, tied up together in a 4-inch square of cheesecloth)
Salt and freshly ground black pepper to taste

Place the chicken in a large soup or stock pot and cover with the water (the pot will be about two-thirds full). Add the onions, garlic, carrots, celery, and bouquet garni, and salt and pepper to taste. Bring to a boil over high heat. Skim off any scum that comes to the surface.

Reduce the heat and simmer approximately 4 hours, skimming regularly. Strain the stock through a strainer. Degrease with a ladle, or by chilling stock, letting fat coagulate on the surface, and spooning off. Use the broth in another recipe, or refrigerate or freeze for later use.

BEEF STOCK
Caldo de Res

Makes 1 quart

Beef stock is used to give a rich flavor base to Oxtail Stew (page 122) and Ajiaco (page 83), a Cuban dish that has been a staple since the days of the Taíno Indians. Beef stock lasts 2 to 3 days in the refrigerator and up to 6 months in the freezer.

Beef stock is nice to have on hand. You may freeze any leftover stock in ice cube trays. Pop out and store in plastic bags, so that you have any amount of stock available when you need it. It will last up to 6 months in the freezer.

3 pounds shin and marrow bones of beef
2 quarts water
1 carrot, chopped
3 stalks celery, chopped
2 tomatoes, chopped

1 medium onion, chopped
1 bouquet garni (made with 1 thyme sprig, 5 black peppercorns, and a parsley sprig, tied up together in a 4-inch square of cheesecloth)

Preheat the oven to 350°F. Place the bones in a roasting pan and bake approximately 30 minutes, until the bones are well browned, turning over once.

Place the browned bones and the remaining ingredients in a large pot. Cover and bring to a boil, then reduce the heat to medium, uncover, and simmer for 3 hours.

Strain the stock through a fine sieve lined with 2 layers of damp cheesecloth. Use the stock in another recipe, or cover and save in refrigerator or freeze until ready to use.

SWEET PLANTAIN SOUP
Sopa de Plátano Maduro

Makes 4 servings

Plantains are the most versatile ingredient in Cuban cooking, and are used to make appetizers, soups, side dishes, and desserts. In this recipe, ripe plantains are pureed into a thick, sweet soup.

1 tablespoon butter
3 large ripe plantains, peeled
* and sliced diagonally into*
* 1½-inch pieces (page 25)*

4 cups water
Juice from ½ lemon
Salt and freshly ground black
* pepper to taste*

In a large sauté pan, melt the butter over medium heat. Add the plantains, flat side down, and sauté until lightly browned on both sides and tender in the middle.

Transfer the plantains to the workbowl of a food processor and puree until smooth. Add 1 cup of the water and transfer to a medium-size saucepan. Whisk in the remaining 3 cups water. Add the lemon juice and place over medium-high heat until the soup reaches a low boil. Reduce the heat to low, cover, and simmer 10 minutes, stirring occasionally. Add salt and pepper to taste, and serve warm.

TRADITIONAL BLACK BEAN SOUP
Sopa Tradicional de Frijoles Negros

Makes 6–8 servings

This dark, rich soup is a classic of Cuban cooking. It is traditionally served with side dishes of rice and chopped-up raw onion, which each person adds to the soup to thicken and sharpen it to his or her personal taste. I like to top it with finely chopped onion and a dollop of sour cream to add a cooling touch.

1 pound dried black beans, cleaned and soaked overnight (page 18)
6 cups water
4 cups chicken stock (page 52)
2 tablespoons olive oil
1 large pork hock, with tough outside skin removed
2 medium onions, finely diced
2 garlic cloves, pressed or finely chopped

2 tablespoons malt vinegar
½ teaspoon ground cumin
1 teaspoon sugar
Salt and freshly ground black pepper to taste
1 onion, finely diced, for topping (optional)
4 tablespoons sour cream for topping (optional)

In a strainer, drain the soaked beans and rinse them lightly under cold running water. Put the beans and the fresh water in a large soup or stock pot (making sure the water covers the beans by at least 1 to 2 inches). Cover and bring to a boil over high heat. When the water has boiled, reduce the heat to low and simmer for at least 2 hours, until the beans are tender enough to be mashed with a spoon.

Remove 1 cup beans and 1 cup liquid, and put in a blender or a food processor. (Use a food mill or sieve if a blender or food processor is unavailable.) Puree the beans and liquid, then return the puree to the pot. Add the chicken stock and return the soup to a simmer over low heat.

In a large skillet, heat the olive oil over medium-high heat. Add the pork hock and brown on both sides. Add the onion and cook until brown. Add the pork hock, onion, and garlic to the soup, cover the pot, and simmer for at least 2 hours. Add the vinegar, cumin, and sugar. Let soup simmer 15 more minutes. Add salt and pepper to taste.

Remove the pork hock. Cut the meat off the bone and stir into the soup. Ladle into serving bowls, and add diced onion and sour cream on top, if desired. Serve hot.

CHILLED YUCA SOUP
Sopa Fría de Yuca

Makes 6–8 servings

Like the plantain, yuca may appear on a Cuban table during any course of a meal. This soup can be prepared up to 2 days before. Store covered in the refrigerator and serve on a day when it's too hot to cook.

4 cups chopped mild onion
4 cups peeled and diced yuca
   (page 28)
7 cups water
½ teaspoon salt

1 cup heavy cream
Salt to taste
Sour cream and chopped scal-
   lion for garnish

In a large saucepan over medium heat, bring the onions, yuca, and water to a boil. Reduce the heat to low, add ½ teaspoon salt, stir, cover, and simmer 20 to 30 minutes. When the yuca is tender, remove from heat and puree in a food processor or blender. Stir in the heavy cream.

Transfer the soup to a large bowl, cover with plastic wrap, and chill in refrigerator 2 to 3 hours. When ready to serve, add salt to taste. Add a dollop of sour cream and a sprinkling of scallion on top of each bowl.

CREAM OF GARLIC SOUP WITH CILANTRO
Sopa de Ajo a la Crema con Cilantro

Makes 8 servings

Don't be scared by the amount of garlic in this soup. The longer garlic is cooked the blander it becomes, until it has a flavor and texture somewhat like those of a potato.

Cilantro is an aromatic herb that has been found in Spanish recipes dating back to the sixteenth century. It is used a great deal in the cuisine of Hispanic countries, including Cuba, and also in Oriental cooking.

When garnishing the bowl before serving, lightly sprinkle with finely chopped cilantro for a beautiful bright-green color and contrast.

2 heads garlic
4 large onions, finely diced
5 cups water
¼ cup butter
2 cups cream
¼ cup chopped fresh cilantro

Separate and peel the garlic cloves. Place the garlic, onions, and water in a large saucepan over medium-high heat and bring to a boil. Reduce the heat to low, cover, and simmer 30 minutes, stirring occasionally.

Remove the soup from the heat and stir well, breaking up the garlic pieces. Stir in the butter until melted. Stir in the cream and serve immediately, topped with chopped cilantro.

GARLIC-TOMATO SOUP
Sopa de Ajo y Tomate

Makes 6–8 servings

This spicy soup reflects the Portuguese influence on Cuban cooking in its heavy use of garlic and parsley. It is similar to the savory tomato soups that are traditional in Portugal.

2 heads garlic
3 tablespoons olive oil
1 pound tomatoes, peeled, seeded,
   and diced
8 cups water
1 teaspoon salt
Freshly ground black pepper to
   taste

1 bay leaf
2 tablespoons chopped fresh
   parsley
½ teaspoon paprika
8 slices Cuban Bread (or any
   other light white bread)
   (page 218)
Olive oil for drizzling

Peel the garlic cloves. In a large saucepan over medium heat, heat the olive oil. Add the garlic cloves and sauté until they begin to brown, approximately 5 minutes. Add the tomatoes and sauté 10 minutes. Add the water, salt, pepper, bay leaf, parsley, and paprika.

Reduce the heat to low, cover, and simmer 30 minutes, stirring occasionally. Remove the lid and simmer 15 minutes, stirring occasionally.

Toast the slices of bread. Ladle the soup into individual bowls and add 1 slice of Cuban bread to each bowl. Drizzle bread with olive oil and serve.

GALICIAN POTAGE
Caldo Gallego

Makes 6–8 servings

The harsh, damp climate of the Galicia region of Spain encouraged the development of hearty, warming foods like this potage. Galician potage traveled to Cuba with the Spanish colonists centuries ago, and is now served in many Cuban restaurants in Miami.

½ pound chorizo or Spanish
   Sausage (page 144)
1 medium onion, diced
¼ cup diced celery,
1 garlic clove, pressed or finely
   chopped

1 pound dried white beans,
   cleaned and soaked overnight
   (page 18)
3 quarts water
Salt and freshly ground black
   pepper to taste

In a large soup or stock pot, cook the sausage over medium-high heat until brown. Drain off and discard approximately half of the excess grease in the pot. Add the onion, celery, and garlic to the pot, and brown over medium heat.

In a strainer, drain the soaked beans and rinse them lightly under cold running water. Add the beans and water to the sausage and vegetable mixture. Bring to a boil over medium-high heat, stirring frequently.

Reduce the heat to medium-low, cover the pot, and simmer for 3 to 4 hours, until the beans are tender. Add salt and pepper to taste, and serve hot.

COLD CUCUMBER
AND AVOCADO SOUP
Sopa Fría de Pepino y Aguacate

Makes 4 servings

This elegant yet easy-to-prepare soup is wonderfully refreshing on torrid days. Since this soup should be served immediately after preparation, make the chicken stock in advance,
allowing it time to chill, and use cold cucumbers and sour
cream.

*2 cucumbers (chilled), peeled
    and seeded*
1 avocado, peeled and pitted
*1⅓ cups chilled chicken stock
    (page 52)*

½ cup sour cream
*Salt and freshly ground black
    pepper to taste*
*Thinly sliced cucumber for
    garnish*

Put the cucumbers and avocado in the workbowl of a food
processor. Blend for 15 seconds, pausing when necessary to
scrape the sides of the bowl. Add the chicken stock and sour
cream and blend for 15 seconds (until the soup is smooth and
without lumps).

Add salt and pepper to taste. Serve cold in chilled bowls or
tureens, with a garnish of floating cucumber slices.

SHRIMP, CORN, AND POTATO SOUP
Sopa de Camarones

Makes 6 servings

This creamy, delectable soup is a traditional Cuban treat. Like many Cuban recipes, it is cooked in one large pot, which simplifies the timing element as well as the cleanup. It is most authentic and flavorful when made with fish stock, but water or chicken stock may be substituted.

1 tablespoon butter
1 tablespoon olive oil
2 medium onions, finely diced
1 garlic clove, pressed or finely chopped
1½ cups chopped, seeded tomatoes
1 cup fish stock (page 51)
1 bay leaf
6 small new potatoes, peeled

3 cups milk
2 ears of corn, shucked and cut crosswise into 3 pieces
1 pound medium raw shrimp, peeled and deveined (pages 26–27)
Salt and freshly ground black pepper to taste

In a large soup or stock pot, heat the butter and oil over medium heat. Add the onions and garlic; cook until slightly brown. Add the tomatoes, fish stock, and bay leaf. Raise the heat to high and bring to a boil.

Add the potatoes and reduce the heat to medium. Cover the pot and simmer about 15 minutes, until the potatoes are tender but not flaking. Stir in the milk, corn, and shrimp and return to a boil. Simmer 10 minutes longer. Add salt and freshly ground black pepper to taste. Serve hot.

WHITE BEAN AND TOMATO SOUP
Sopa de Frijoles Blancos con Tomate

Makes 10 servings

The white beans against the red broth make this a very attractive soup to serve to guests, especially if you add a green garnish such as fresh parsley or cilantro.

2 tablespoons butter
1 pork hock, with tough outside skin removed
1 medium onion, diced
6 cups water
2½ cups chicken stock (page 52)

1 cup small white beans, cleaned and soaked overnight (page 18)
3 cups peeled and seeded tomatoes
½ cup white wine
Chopped fresh parsley or cilantro for garnish

In a sauté pan, melt the butter over medium heat. Add the ham hock and sauté until brown on both sides. Add the onion and sauté until slightly brown. Add 2 cups of the water to the sauté pan and stir, scraping the bottom of the pan, until ingredients are well combined. Remove from the stove and set aside.

In a large soup or stock pot, bring the remaining 4 cups of water and the chicken stock to a boil over high heat. In a strainer, drain the soaked beans and rinse them under cold running water. Add the beans, tomatoes, and wine, and the ham hock, onion, and juice from the sauté pan to the pot. Reduce the heat to medium. Cover and simmer 2½ to 3 hours.

With a slotted spoon, remove the ham hock from the pot, allow to cool slightly before handling, then cut the meat from the bone. Discard the bone and add the meat to the soup. Garnish the soup with chopped fresh parsley or cilantro and serve hot.

CONCH CHOWDER
Sopa de Cobo

Makes 4–6 servings

This Cuban-Floridian chowder includes side pork (also called streak of lean), which is uncured bacon that is available at most butcher shops. When I serve this chowder, I put a bottle of cream sherry on the table and encourage guests to splash a little over their soup. See page 21 for information on purchasing, cleaning, and pounding conch.

2 strips side pork
1 tablespoon butter
2 cups finely chopped onion
1 large green bell pepper, seeded, deribbed, and chopped
2 cups peeled and seeded tomatoes in juice
4 large potatoes, peeled and chopped

2 quarts water
A few dashes of Tabasco sauce
1 pound conch meat, pounded and cut into small pieces (page 21)
Salt and freshly ground black pepper to taste
Chopped fresh parsley for garnish

In a large soup or stock pot, brown the side pork over medium heat. Remove the pork from the pot and set aside. Add the butter, onions, and pepper to the pot, and sauté until soft. Crumble the side pork and return it to the pot. Add the tomatoes, potatoes, water, and Tabasco sauce. Bring the soup to a boil over medium-high heat.

Add the conch meat to the pot. Cover and simmer over medium heat for 1 hour. Add salt and pepper to taste. Serve hot, with a garnish of chopped fresh parsley.

CHICKEN AND RICE SOUP
Sopa de Pollo con Arroz

Makes 8–10 servings

In Cuban kitchens, leftover rice is often used in chicken and rice soup. This recipe, which features homemade chicken stock that can be pre-prepared, is simple and quick, yet it tastes as if a lot of love and care has gone into it.

10 cups chicken stock (page 52)

1 pound boneless, skinless chicken breasts, cut into 1-inch strips

¼ cup butter

2 large onions, chopped

6 celery stalks, chopped

6 carrots, peeled and chopped into 1-inch pieces

Salt and freshly ground black pepper to taste

2 cups cooked long-grain white rice (page 95)

Minced fresh parsley for garnish

In a large soup or stock pot, bring the chicken stock to a boil. Add the chicken, and reduce the heat to simmer.

In a small sauté pan, melt the butter over medium heat. Add the onions, celery, and carrots and sauté until the onions and celery are tender.

Add the vegetables to the pot and simmer about 30 minutes. Add salt and pepper to taste. Add the rice and simmer 5 minutes. Serve hot, garnished with sprinklings of parsley.

RED BEAN SOUP
Sopa de Frijoles Colorados

Makes 8 servings

Most foods taste best fresh, but this spicy Cuban soup actually gains in texture and pungency if it is made a day in advance.

2 tablespoons butter
2 tablespoons olive oil
1 large onion, chopped
1 large carrot, peeled and
   chopped
2 tablespoons minced fresh
   parsley
3 garlic cloves, pressed or
   finely chopped

6 cups water
1½ pounds dried red kidney
   beans, cleaned and soaked
   overnight (page 18)
1 medium-size ham hock, with
   tough outside skin removed
3 cups peeled and seeded tomatoes
Sprigs of fresh cilantro for
   garnish

In a large soup or stock pot, melt the butter with the olive oil over medium heat. Add the onions, carrots, parsley, and garlic. Cover and cook until the onions are tender.

Add the water and bring to a boil over high heat. In a strainer, drain the soaked beans and rinse them lightly under cold running water. Add the beans and ham hock to the soup pot, and bring back to a boil. Add the tomatoes, then cover and reduce the heat to medium-low. Simmer approximately 1½ hours, until the beans are tender.

Remove the ham hock. Pour the soup through a strainer, reserving the liquid in another pot. Transfer the solids to the workbowl of a food processor. Process until smooth, stopping when necessary to scrape the sides of the bowl.

Return the puree and liquid to the soup pot. Cover and simmer over low heat. Cut the meat from the hambone into small pieces. Discard the bone and put the meat into the soup. Stir well. Garnish with cilantro and serve hot.

SWEET AND SPICY CALABAZA SOUP
Sopa Agridulce de Calabaza

Makes 4–6 servings

Calabaza, or Cuban squash, has green skin and orange flesh. Calabaza can be as small as a honeydew, but often grow to be too huge to carry easily, so they are sold in chunks and large crescent slices in Hispanic markets. See page 19 for information on purchasing and handling calabaza.

1 calabaza, approximately 3
    pounds, or a 3-pound piece
    of calabaza
4 tablespoons butter
2 large onions, diced
2 teaspoons ground coriander
1 teaspoon ground cumin

½ teaspoon ground white pepper
1 teaspoon salt
3 cups chicken stock (page 52)
1 ripe plantain, peeled and cut
    into ¼-inch slices (page 25)
1 cup apple juice

Preheat the oven to 350°F. Cut the calabaza in half (if it is whole), then remove and discard the seeds (page 19). Place the calabaza flesh side down on a cookie sheet and bake approximately 30 minutes.

While the pumpkin is baking, melt the butter over medium heat in a large soup pot. Add the onions, coriander, cumin, pepper, and salt. Cover and cook until the onions are soft, about 20 minutes.

Add the chicken stock to the pot and bring to a boil over high heat. When the soup is boiling, add the sliced plantain. Cover the pot and reduce the heat to medium. Simmer 10 minutes.

Remove the calabaza from the oven and allow to cool enough to handle. Scoop out the calabaza flesh, breaking it into small pieces, and add it to the soup. Add the apple juice and simmer for ½ hour, until the plantain is tender.

Pour the soup through a strainer, reserving the liquid in a large pot. Transfer the solid ingredients from the strainer to the workbowl of a food processor. Process until smooth, stopping when necessary to scrape the sides of the bowl.

Return the puree and liquid to the pot. Cover and simmer over low heat until hot. If you wish to thicken the soup, uncover and cook over low heat, stirring frequently, until the desired consistency is reached. Serve hot.

VEGETABLE SOUP WITH LENTILS AND RICE
Sopa de Vegetales con Lentejas y Arroz

Makes 10 servings

While this soup is nutritious enough to provide a full meal, the lightness of the broth makes it a suitable first course for a special dinner. Be careful not to overcook the lentils or they will turn mushy. They are done as soon as they are tender yet firm enough to hold their shape.

6 cups chicken stock (page 52)
3 cups water
1½ cups lentils, rinsed
3 cups peeled and seeded tomatoes
3 carrots, peeled and cut into ¼-inch pieces
1 medium onion, chopped
1 celery stalk, chopped
3 garlic cloves, minced
3 fresh basil leaves, or ½ teaspoon dried basil
1 fresh thyme sprig, or ½ teaspoon dried thyme
1 sprig fresh oregano, or ½ teaspoon dried and crumbled oregano
1 bay leaf
½ cup minced fresh parsley
2 cups cooked long-grain white rice (page 95)
¼ cup white wine
Salt and freshly ground black pepper to taste

In a large soup or stock pot, combine the chicken stock, water, and lentils. Bring to a boil over high heat. Cover, reduce the heat to simmer, and cook 15 minutes.

While the lentils are cooking, place the tomatoes and juice in a large mixing bowl. Using your hands, squeeze the tomatoes through your fingers, breaking them apart into small pieces.

When lentils have cooked 15 minutes, add the tomatoes, carrots, onion, celery, garlic, basil, thyme, oregano, bay leaf, and parsley. Raise the heat to high and bring to a boil. Reduce the heat to medium and simmer, covered, for another 15 minutes, stirring frequently. Remove the bay leaf and add the rice. Let simmer 5 minutes, until the rice is plump. Add the wine and stir thoroughly. Add salt and pepper to taste, and serve hot.

FRUITS AND VEGETABLES

Fresh salads and green vegetables rarely appear on Cuban tables and fresh fruit is usually eaten as an appetizer, snack, or dessert. However, there are a number of marvelous cooked root vegetable and plantain dishes that are served as side dishes at lunch and dinner time.

Plantains have multiple personalities: They are starchy when green and unripe, semisweet when yellow and mottled, and sweet when brownish-black and fully ripe. They are technically fruits (members of the banana family), but are often treated more like vegetables: fried, baked, and mashed. Cubans enjoy plantains in a number of variations, which you will learn to prepare in this chapter.

Yuca, which is also called cassava, is another staple of Cuban cooking. This root vegetable is deeply associated with Cuban heritage, having formed the basis of the diet of the Taíno Indians and later been adopted by the Spanish settlers and their African slaves.

Boniato, or Cuban sweet potato, is another widely eaten vegetable. It is more delicate and less sweet than the American sweet potato, with a unique and subtle flavor. Calabaza, which are large Cuban squash, are also cooked into hearty side dishes.

For instructions on selecting, storing, and preparing plantains, yuca, boniatos, and calabaza, see the Ingredients chapter.

FRIED SWEET PLANTAINS
Plátanos Maduros Fritos

Makes 4–6 servings

Fried plantains are a standard Cuban side dish and are often served with rice and beans and entrées of meat or fish. You can purchase ripe plantains or ripen green ones (see page 25).

¼ cup butter
1 tablespoon olive oil
3 ripe plantains, peeled and cut
   diagonally into 1-inch slices
   (page 25)

Juice from ½ lemon
Salt to taste

In a large skillet, melt the butter with the olive oil over medium heat. Add the plantain slices and fry approximately 4 minutes on each side, moving the slices with a spatula occasionally to prevent sticking.

Remove the plantains from the skillet with a slotted spoon and let drain on paper towels. Transfer to a large, warm serving platter, sprinkle with lemon juice and salt, and serve warm.

MASHED GREEN PLANTAINS
Fufú

Makes 4–6 servings

Green, unripe plantains are shorter and wider than the larger, riper, yellow or brown variety. They taste more like a vegetable than a fruit, and lack the sweetness of ripe plantains.

5 small green plantains (page 26)
¼ cup butter, softened

½ cup milk
Salt and freshly ground black pepper to taste

Place the plantains in a large pot. Fill the pot with enough water to cover the plantains, cover the pot, and bring the water to a boil over medium-high heat. Simmer 30 minutes, until the plantains are tender.

Drain in a colander and let the plantains cool enough to handle. Peel the plantains and place in a large mixing bowl. Chop the plantains into small pieces, then mash with a potato masher.

Add the butter and mix well. Add the milk, and salt and pepper to taste. If the mixture is dry, moisten slightly with warm milk and more butter, if you wish. Serve warm.

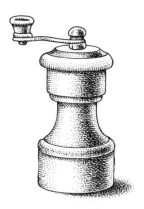

TOSTONES

Makes 4 servings

This traditional side dish and snack is a favorite among Cuban children, who playfully flatten the *tostones* with the palms of their hands before eating them.

Vegetable oil for frying   *Salt to taste*
1 large green plantain, peeled
and cut into 1-inch diago-
nal slices (page 26)

Fill a deep fryer halfway with oil and heat to 375°F. (If a deep fryer is unavailable, fill a large skillet a third full with oil and heat over medium-high heat.) Deep-fry the plantain slices for 5 minutes, until they begin to brown. (If using a skillet, fry for 5 minutes on each side.)

Remove the plantain with a slotted spoon and let drain on paper towels. When the plantain slices are slightly cooled, place a paper towel on top of them and flatten to about half their size with the palm of your hand.

Return the plantain to the fryer (or skillet) and fry until golden brown (3 to 4 minutes). Remove and let drain again on paper towels. Sprinkle with salt to taste, and serve warm.

YUCA WITH GARLIC SAUCE
Yuca con Mojo

Makes 4 servings

This recipe offers a simple and traditional way to enjoy yuca. In Miami, there has recently arisen an amusing play on the name of this vegetable. "Yuca" is an acronym for Young Upscale Cuban-Americans.

1½ pounds yuca, peeled and
  halved (page 28), cut into
  bite-size cubes
1 teaspoon salt

5 cloves garlic, minced
Juice from 1 lemon
½ cup olive oil

Place the yuca in a large saucepan and add enough water to cover it by at least 2 inches. Add the salt and bring to a boil over medium-high heat. Reduce the heat to low, cover, and cook 30 minutes, until the yuca is tender but still intact.

Drain the yuca through a strainer, then return it to the saucepan. Toss with the garlic, lemon juice, and olive oil. Raise the heat to medium and toss gently for 5 minutes, until lightly browned. Transfer to a warm serving platter and serve.

CALABAZA FRITTERS
Frituras de Calabaza

Makes 12 fritters

Because calabaza can be so enormous that it would be difficult to carry a whole one home or use it up, it may be more
practical to purchase a large slice in the market.

1½ pounds calabaza   ¼ teaspoon nutmeg
2 tablespoons butter   1½ cups flour
1 egg, slightly beaten   Vegetable oil for frying
½ cup sugar   Salt to taste

Cut calabaza flesh into 1-inch pieces (page 19) and place
in a large saucepan with enough water to cover. Bring to a
boil over medium-high heat. Cover, reduce the heat to low,
and simmer 20 minutes.

Drain the calabaza in a strainer, then place it in a bowl and
mash. Measure 1½ cups mashed calabaza into a large bowl.
Add the butter, egg and sugar, and mix until the butter is
melted and well blended. Add the nutmeg and stir, then add
the flour ½ cup at a time, mixing well.

Heat the oil in a deep fryer to 375°F. or heat oil in a deep
skillet, no more than halfway full, to 375°. Drop the dough, 1
tablespoon at a time, into the hot oil. Fry fritters a few at a
time until lightly browned (about 4 to 5 minutes). Remove
and place on paper towels to drain. Sprinkle lightly with salt,
and serve warm.

BONIATO CHIPS
Boniato Frito

Makes 4 servings

These fried boniato chips are delicious as a snack, or they can be served as a side dish with pork dishes.

4 boniatos (page 18)
Olive oil for frying
Salt to taste

Preheat the oven to 400°F. Scrub and dry the boniatos, pierce them several times with a fork, place them on the middle rack of the oven, and bake for 45 minutes. Remove from the oven and allow to cool, then slice lengthwise into ½-inch thick slices, discarding the end pieces.

In a large skillet, heat ⅛ inch of oil over medium-high heat. Place the boniatos, 8 to 10 at a time, in hot oil and cook 2 minutes on each side, until lightly browned. Remove with a fork and place on paper towels to drain. Transfer the chips to a serving platter, salt to taste, and serve immediately.

BONIATO DUMPLINGS
Rellenos de Boniato

Makes 6 servings

You can make these dumplings with leftover boniatos that were baked or mashed, or, of course, you can start with fresh ones. They can be served with a poultry entrée to add color as well as being a nice accompaniment.

Before cooking boniatos, scrub them thoroughly.

To bake: Preheat the oven to 350°F., drain the boniatos and pierce them with a fork several times, then wrap them in aluminum foil, place on the oven rack, and bake for 1 hour.

To boil: Place in a pot with enough water to cover, and boil for 15 to 20 minutes. After cooking, allow the boniatos to cool to room temperature, then peel and mash with a fork or potato masher.

3 cups cold, mashed boniatos (made from approximately 2 pounds boniatos, approximately 4 to 6 boniatos) (see Headnote)
Flour for dusting work surface
1 cup flour

2 egg yolks
1 garlic clove, pressed or finely chopped
2 teaspoons salt
¼ cup melted butter
Salt and freshly ground black pepper to taste

Place the boniatos in center of a lightly floured working surface. Work in the flour, egg yolks, and garlic by hand. Roll into 1-inch balls. Lightly press down on the tops of the finished balls with the tines of a fork to flatten slightly.

Fill a large pot halfway with water, add the 2 teaspoons salt, and bring to a boil over medium-high heat. Drop 6 to 8 dumplings at a time into the pot and cook until they float to the top, approximately 5 minutes.

Remove the dumplings with a slotted spoon and let drain on paper towels. Just before serving, pour the melted butter over the dumplings and sprinkle with salt and pepper.

RUM-GLAZED BONIATOS
Boniato Glaceado con Ron

Makes 8–10 servings

This recipe is irresistible to anyone with a sweet tooth. It is an excellent side dish to serve with a juicy loin of pork or a roasted chicken.

3 pounds boniatos (page 18)	*2 tablespoons light brown sugar*
¼ cup melted butter	*3 tablespoons dark rum*
Salt and freshly ground black pepper to taste	

Preheat the oven to 425°F. Scrub the boniatos, then place them in a large pot with enough water to cover. Bring to a boil over medium-high heat and cook 15 to 20 minutes, until the boniatos are barely tender.

Drain and rinse the boniatos under cold water. When cool enough to handle, peel and slice into ¼-inch rounds (the skins should come off easily with paring knife).

Use 1 tablespoon of the melted butter to grease a shallow glass baking dish. Arrange the boniatos, slightly overlapping, in the dish and drizzle with the remaining butter. Sprinkle with salt, pepper, and brown sugar, and cover with aluminum foil. Lower the oven to 350°F. and bake for 25 minutes. Uncover, raise the temperature back to 425°F., and bake 10 to 15 minutes longer.

Just before serving, warm the rum in a small saucepan. Drizzle the rum evenly over the boniatos, and serve.

AJIACO

Makes 8 servings

Ajiaco is the ultimate *criollo* dish—*criollo* meaning born in Cuba rather than being of Spanish origin. *Ajiaco* is a Taíno Indian word, and was originally a thick vegetable soup-stew which the Taínos ate with cassava bread. The Spaniards added beef, sausage, and other ingredients, and there are now many variations of this stew. It makes a hearty, country-style meal when served with Cassava Bread (page 217) and rice and beans (see Rice and Beans chapter).

¼ cup olive oil
1½ pounds beef stew meat
1½ pounds chorizo or Spanish
　Sausage (page 144)
1 large onion, coarsely chopped
4 cloves garlic, minced
2 green bell peppers, seeded,
　deribbed, and coarsely chopped
2 cups water
2 cups beef stock (page 54)
½ cup dry red wine
2 ears of corn, husked and
　quartered

2 green plantains, peeled and
　quartered (page 26)
1 medium-size yuca, peeled and
　coarsely chopped (page 28)
1 cup malanga, peeled and
　chopped into 1-inch cubes
　(page 23)
4 tomatoes, quartered
½ cup minced fresh parsley
Salt and freshly ground black
　pepper to taste

In a large soup pot, heat the olive oil over medium heat. When hot, add the stew meat and sausage and stir until brown. Add the onion, garlic, and green pepper, and sauté until tender but not brown.

Add the water, beef stock, and red wine. Raise the heat to high and bring to a boil, stirring occasionally. When just at a boil, add the corn, plantains, yuca, malanga, and tomatoes. Stir well, cover, and reduce the heat to medium-low.

Let the ajiaco simmer 30 minutes, stirring occasionally. Stir in the parsley and salt and pepper to taste, and serve.

FRESH CORN AND RED PEPPER TAMALES
Tamales de Maíz Tierno y Ajíes

Makes 15 tamales

Cuban children are often asked to husk the corn for tamales, which are a favorite treat among young and old alike. Tamales are cooked slowly over steam, wrapped in either corn husks or banana leaves. I recommend using corn husks, because they are more readily available. A cooling dollop of sour cream sprinkled with paprika is a pleasing addition to a hot tamale.

These tamales can be served as an appetizer or as a main course with a rice-and-bean dish.

About 10 ears of corn (enough to yield 45 corn husks and 2 cups fresh corn kernels)
½ cup red bell pepper, seeded, deribbed, and diced
¾ cup sour cream

1 cup milk
¼ cup cornmeal
½ teaspoon salt
½ teaspoon cayenne pepper
Sour cream and paprika to garnish (optional)

Remove the husks from the corn, saving the large inner ones and discarding the very outer and very small inside husks. (You'll need 3 husks for each tamale.) In a large ceramic bowl, soak the leaves in enough hot water to cover and set aside.

With a sharp knife, remove the kernels of corn from the cobs, saving the juices. In a large mixing bowl, mix 2 cups of corn and juices with the red pepper, sour cream, milk, cornmeal, salt, and cayenne pepper.

Drain the corn husks through a colander and pat dry with paper towels. Place approximately ¼ cup (4 tablespoons) of corn filling onto a husk, lengthwise. Then bring the top and bottom ends to the center, slightly overlapping. Wrap another husk around, it lengthwise, forming a cylindrical shape. Use one more husk to seal and secure the shape by wrapping the opposite way. Using butcher string, tie securely crosswise and knot.

Place the tamales in a steamer (or a pan with a rack) over simmering water and steam 1 hour. Remove with a slotted spatula and cut the strings off. Allow to cool slightly before serving. Add a dollop of sour cream and sprinkle with paprika if desired.

PEPPERS STUFFED WITH SPANISH SAUSAGE, RICE, AND TOMATO
Ajíes Rellenos con Chorizo, Arroz, y Tomate

Makes 8 servings

In Spanish and Cuban kitchens, peppers are stuffed with an amazing variety of ingredients. These spicy stuffed peppers can be served as an entrée, or as a side dish with a loin of pork or roast chicken.

2½ cups water
1 teaspoon salt
1 small bay leaf
1 cup long-grain white rice
2 tablespoons butter
1 tablespoon olive oil
1 garlic clove, chopped
1 cup minced onion

2 cups peeled and seeded tomatoes
1 pound chorizo or Spanish
Sausage (page 144)
8 medium green bell peppers,
seeded, deribbed, and cut in
half lengthwise
1 teaspoon tomato paste

Preheat the oven to 350°F. In a large pot, bring 2 cups of the water and the salt and bay leaf to a boil over high heat. Add the rice, cover, and reduce the heat to medium. Simmer for 15 minutes, stirring occasionally to be sure the rice doesn't stick. When the rice is barely cooked, set aside.

In a medium-size sauté pan, melt the butter in with the oil over medium heat. Add the garlic and onions and cook until the onions are translucent, 3 to 5 minutes. Meanwhile, place tomatoes in a mixing bowl and break up with your fingers to crush them. Add to the sauté pan and cook until hot. Strain any excess water from the rice. Add the tomato mixture to the rice and stir.

In the sauté pan, brown the sausage over medium heat. Drain the excess grease from the sausage on paper towels and stir the sausage into the tomato-and-rice mixture.

Place the peppers in a shallow baking dish and fill with the stuffing mixture.

In a small mixing bowl, mix the tomato paste and the remaining ½ cup water and pour around the outside of the peppers.

Bake for 45 minutes, basting twice with the tomato paste mixture. Remove from the oven and serve warm.

VEGETABLE AND CHEESE OMELET
Tortilla Española con Vegetales y Queso

Makes 2 omelets

In Cuban cooking, cheese is not used very often. When it is an ingredient, as in this recipe, a sharp white cheese is usually used. This omelet is simple to prepare, but for it to be successful, you need to be careful not to overbeat or overcook the eggs.

4 eggs, at room temperature
1 teaspoon olive oil
¼ cup chopped onion
¼ cup chopped green bell pepper
¼ cup peeled, seeded, and chopped tomatoes
1 garlic clove, minced
1 small potato, peeled, boiled, and sliced

Salt and freshly ground black pepper to taste
2 tablespoons clarified butter (see Note)
¼ cup shredded sharp white cheese (such as a white Cheddar)

Lightly beat 2 of the eggs in a small mixing bowl and 2 in another. Set aside.

In a small sauté pan, heat the olive oil over medium heat. Add the onion, green pepper, tomato, garlic, and potato and sauté until tender, approximately 4 minutes. Remove from the heat, add salt and pepper to taste, and set aside.

In a 7-inch omelet pan or a small sauté pan, heat 1 table-spoon of the clarified butter over medium-high heat. When the pan is hot, pour in 2 of the lightly beaten eggs and move the pan back and forth over heat to cook the eggs, approximately 1 minute. Using a spatula, transfer the eggs to a serving plate by sliding them from the pan, gently guiding them with a spatula. Sprinkle with 2 tablespoons of the shredded cheese. Place 2 tablespoons of the filling in the center of the eggs, then fold in half.

Repeat the process with the other two eggs. Use the remaining filling to garnish the tops of the omelets, and serve.

Note: To clarify butter: Clarifying butter is easiest when done in batches of ½ pound or more. Place the butter in a saucepan over low heat and let sit till melted. Do not let it simmer. When butter is melted, skim foam from top. There should now be clarified butter that has risen to the top and milk solids settled on the bottom. Carefully, so as not to stir or unsettle the bottom, pour butter into a small saucepan. When you get down to the milk solids, stop and discard them. Keep clarified butter warm and use when needed.

AVOCADOS WITH VINAIGRETTE
Aguacate a la Vinagreta

Makes 6 servings

Avocados grow wild in Cuba, on tall, stately trees with dark green leaves. Wild avocados are small, only about 3 inches long, but cultivation has given us larger varieties.

When sliced and exposed to air, avocados rapidly begin to turn brown in color. For this reason, I recommend making the vinaigrette first and cutting the avocados right before serving. Another way to avoid discoloration is to sprinkle the avocados with lemon juice.

¾ cup olive oil
¼ cup lemon juice
½ teaspoon grainy mustard
2 tablespoons honey

Salt and freshly ground black
pepper to taste
3 large ripe avocados

In a small ceramic bowl, mix together the olive oil, lemon juice, mustard, honey, salt and pepper.

Slice the avocados in half lengthwise and remove the center pit. Slice each half in half (making 4 pieces from each avocado). Carefully peel the skin off each piece. Slice the pieces lengthwise into ⅛-inch-wide slices.

Place the pieces on a serving platter, drizzle the vinaigrette over them, and serve immediately.

RICE AND BEANS

When one thinks of Cuban cooking, a steaming pot of hearty black beans and rice probably comes to mind. Rice and beans have been staples of the Cuban diet since the seventeenth century, when the Spanish colonists brought them to Cuba. There they flourished in the warm climate and became major crops. Cuban-Americans have continued the rice-and-beans tradition.

Beans, which are members of the legume family of plants, form a complete protein when served with rice. They are not only less expensive than meat, but a healthier form of protein as well: they are low in fat and rich in vitamins.

There is only one problem with eating beans. They can produce intestinal gas, because of the sugars contained in the beans, called oligosaccarides, which need to be broken down so the body can properly process them. There are many ways to deal with this problem; however, I find the most effective method is to cook the beans as we recommend in this book by soaking beforehand. This cuts down on the cooking time and helps with the problem of flatulence. If you are short of time, you may cook the beans without soaking them, as also directed in this book (page 17).

LONG-GRAIN WHITE RICE
Arroz Blanco de Grano Largo

Makes 6 servings (3 cups cooked rice)

Rice is served nearly every day in most Cuban households, as a side dish at lunch or dinner, often accompanied by black beans.

Rice that is cooked and stored properly is very easy to use again. You can use it in most dishes that call for uncooked rice, and it is excellent for rice pudding.

Cooked rice can be stored in a sealed container in the refrigerator for up to 10 days. To reheat and soften it, add 2 tablespoons of water for every cup of rice. Fluff it with a fork as you heat it over low heat.

2 cups water
1 teaspoon salt
1 cup long-grain white rice

In a medium-size saucepan over high heat, bring the water and salt to a boil. Add the rice, turn the heat down to medium-low, and cook, covered, approximately 18 minutes, stirring occasionally, until the rice has absorbed all the liquid. Remove from the heat and serve, or use in another recipe.

BLACK BEANS
Frijoles Negros

Makes 6–8 servings (4 cups cooked beans)

Black beans are the most common and frequently used beans in Cuba. Often there will be leftover beans, for which there are many uses. You may either freeze or refrigerate beans. They will keep 2 to 3 days when placed in a small covered bowl in the refrigerator. When frozen they will keep up to 6 months. To freeze, pack in small 1-to-2-cup plastic containers, so that you won't have to defrost more than you need to use. Beans may only be frozen once.

Treat leftover beans as you would just-cooked beans. If a recipe calls for hot beans, simply heat defrosted beans over medium heat with a little extra water to help keep them moist and prevent them from sticking to the pan. Red and white beans that are left over can also be stored and reheated in the same manner.

1 pound dried black beans, cleaned and soaked overnight (page 18)
2 ounces salt pork (1 thick slice)
1 small onion, peeled and left whole

2 tablespoons butter
2 garlic cloves, pressed or minced
1 large onion, diced
1 teaspoon salt (optional)

Drain the soaked beans in a strainer and rinse them lightly under cold running water. Place them in a large pot with enough fresh water to cover. Add the salt pork and small onion and bring to a boil over high heat. Lower the heat to medium and simmer for 1½ hours, until the beans are tender (adding more water if necessary).

In a large saucepan, melt the butter over medium heat. Add the garlic and onion, and sauté about 4 to 6 minutes, until translucent. Add 1 cup of the cooked beans to the butter-vegetable mixture and mash together, then add the mixture to the bean pot. Mix together, season with salt to taste, and serve. If using in another recipe, see whether it calls for cooked and drained beans. You may not want mashed beans added for some recipes.

BLACK BEANS AND RICE
Moros y Cristianos

Makes 6–8 servings

Black beans and rice, or Moros y Cristianos, is a classic Cuban recipe. It is usually served as a side dish with meat and fried plantains. The Spanish name refers to the conflict between the dark-skinned Moors, who invaded Spain in the eighth century and dominated the country for hundreds of years, and the white-skinned Christians, who eventually regained control of their homeland. On menus in Cuban-American restaurants, this name is often shortened to Moros rice.

2 tablespoons olive oil
1 medium onion, diced
2 garlic cloves, crushed
½ cup seeded, deribbed, and chopped green bell pepper
2 medium tomatoes, peeled, seeded, and chopped

2 cups cooked black beans (page 96)
1 cup chicken stock (page 52)
1 cup long-grain white rice
2 cups water
Salt and freshly ground black pepper to taste

In a large pot, heat the oil over medium heat. Add the onion, garlic, and green pepper, and sauté 4 to 6 minutes. Add the tomatoes, black beans, and chicken stock. Let simmer for approximately 5 minutes, stirring frequently, until heated through.

Add the rice and water, cover, and cook over low heat, stirring occasionally, for 15 to 20 minutes, until the rice is tender. Add salt and pepper to taste, and serve hot.

YELLOW RICE
Arroz Amarillo

Makes 6 servings

In this recipe, the yellow rice gets its color from saffron, an Indian spice made from the dried stamens of the crocus flower. Since this exotic spice is rather expensive, Cuban cooks sometimes use turmeric, with its bright yellow coloring, instead.

2¼ cups water
2¼ cups chicken stock (page 52)
½ teaspoon crumbled saffron threads

¼ cup butter
½ teaspoon salt
2 cups long-grain white rice

In a large pot, bring the water, chicken stock, saffron, butter, and salt to a boil over medium-high heat. Add the rice and stir. Cover the pot, reduce the heat to medium-low, and simmer 20 minutes, stirring occasionally. Serve when the rice is tender.

YELLOW RICE AND PEAS
Arroz Amarillo con Petit Pois

Makes 6 servings

Although saffron is traditionally used to make yellow rice, many Cuban cooks save money by using chicken stock instead, as is done in this recipe. Fresh peas taste best in this side dish, but frozen petit pois are sometimes substituted.

1/4 cup olive oil
1 medium onion, chopped
2 garlic cloves, minced
2½ cups chicken stock (page 52)
1 cup long-grain white rice

Juice from ½ lemon
1 cup fresh peas or frozen petit pois
Salt and freshly ground black pepper to taste

In a large saucepan, heat the olive oil over medium heat. Add the onion and garlic, and sauté 4 to 6 minutes, until translucent. Stir in the chicken stock and raise the heat to medium-high.

When the stock comes to a boil, add the rice, lemon juice, and peas if you are using fresh peas (if you are using frozen peas, add during the last 10 minutes of cooking, since they require less cooking time). Reduce the heat to medium-low and simmer, covered, 20 to 25 minutes, stirring occasionally, until all the liquid is absorbed and the rice is tender. Serve hot.

RUM-FLAVORED BLACK BEANS AND RICE
Arroz y Frijoles Negros con Sabor a Ron

Makes 10–12 servings

The rum, combined with the meaty taste of the black beans, adds a surprising and distinctive flavor to this variation of traditional Moros y Cristianos.

2 large onions, chopped
4 garlic cloves, minced
1/2 cup chopped celery
1/2 cup chopped carrots
1/4 cup olive oil
8 1/2 cups water
1 pound dried black beans, cleaned and soaked overnight (page 18)

1/2 teaspoon black pepper
1/4 cup chopped fresh parsley
2 cups long-grain white rice
1/4 cup dark rum
1 teaspoon salt
1/4 cup chopped fresh parsley for garnish (or 5 parsley sprigs)

In a large saucepan, sauté the onions, garlic, celery, and carrots in the olive oil over medium heat for 4 to 6 minutes, until the onions are translucent. Add 4 1/2 cups of the water and bring to a boil.

Drain the beans and add them, with the pepper and parsley, to the saucepan. Cover, reduce the heat to medium-low, and simmer for 1 1/2 hours, until the beans are tender. Stir occasionally and add water if necessary.

While the beans and vegetables are cooking, in a large pot, bring the remaining 4 cups water to a boil over high heat. Add the rice, reduce the heat to medium, cover, and simmer 18 to 20 minutes, stirring occasionally.

When the beans are tender, mix in the rum and salt. Place the rice on a warm serving platter, drain any excess liquid if necessary and add black beans on top. Garnish with parsley, and serve hot.

MARINATED BLACK BEAN SALAD
Ensalada de Frijoles Negros

Makes 8–10 servings

This salad is a delightful way to enjoy beans on a hot day. It is a practical picnic or buffet item, as it can be prepared ahead of time.

8 cups water
1 pound black beans, cleaned and soaked overnight (page 18)
½ cup olive oil
¼ cup balsamic vinegar
1 tablespoon grainy Dijon mustard

1 medium red onion, chopped
2 medium tomatoes, peeled, seeded, and diced
Salt and freshly ground black pepper to taste
1 red onion, thinly sliced, for garnish (optional)

In a large pot, bring the water to a boil over high heat. Drain the soaked beans in a strainer and rinse them lightly under cold running water. Add the beans to the pot, stir, cover, and reduce the heat to medium-low. Simmer approximately 1½ hours, until the beans are tender, stirring occasionally and adding water if necessary. Drain the beans in a colander and let cool at room temperature.

In a small bowl, mix together the olive oil, vinegar, and mustard. Set aside. Place the beans, onion, and tomato in a large bowl. Drizzle with dressing and toss. Add salt and pepper to taste.

Place in the refrigerator to chill. Serve cold, garnished with thinly sliced rings of red onion if desired.

SPICY BLACK BEANS WITH TOMATOES, ONIONS, AND PEPPERS
Frijoles Negros Picantes con Tomates, Cebollas, y Ajíes

Makes 4–6 servings

The onions and peppers make this a perfect accompaniment to steak or barbecued chicken. Leftover or freshly cooked black beans can be used (see page 96).

2 tablespoons butter
2 tablespoons olive oil
1 medium onion, chopped
2 garlic cloves, minced or pressed
1 green bell pepper, seeded, deribbed, and chopped
1 red bell pepper, seeded, deribbed, and chopped
2 cups cooked black beans (page 96)

½ teaspoon salt or to taste
6 fresh plum tomatoes, peeled, seeded, and chopped
2 tablespoons olive oil
¼ cup freshly chopped cilantro or parsley
¼ teaspoon ground cayenne pepper
4–5 parsley sprigs for garnish

In a large sauté pan, heat the butter and olive oil over medium heat. Add the onion, garlic, and green and red peppers, and sauté 4–6 minutes, until onions are translucent and vegetables are tender.

Add the black beans and salt to taste. Add tomatoes and olive oil. Let cook another 5 minutes, until hot throughout. Add cilantro and mix well. Add cayenne pepper to taste and serve hot, garnished with sprigs of parsley.

RED BEANS AND RICE
Arroz y Frijoles Colorados

Makes 8 servings

This zesty dish uses red beans, also known as kidney beans, which are grown in Cuba and are popular throughout the West Indies.

2 strips side pork (page 27)
2 garlic cloves, minced
1 large onion, chopped
1 cup dried red beans, cleaned and soaked overnight (page 18)

4½ cups chicken stock (page 52)
1 teaspoon salt
¼ cup chopped fresh parsley
2 cups long-grain white rice

In a medium-size sauté pan, brown the side pork on both sides over medium heat. Remove and set aside on paper towels to drain and cool. Add the garlic and onion to the pork grease and sauté 4 to 6 minutes, until translucent.

Drain the soaked beans in a strainer and rinse them lightly under cold running water. In a medium-size pot, bring the chicken stock, salt, parsley, and beans to a boil. Reduce the heat to medium, cover, and simmer for 30 minutes. Crumble the pork into the stock, then add onions, garlic, and rice. Cover, reduce the heat to medium-low, and simmer 20 to 30 minutes, stirring occasionally, until the beans and rice are tender. Serve warm.

SWEET BAKED WHITE BEANS AND PORK
Frijoles Blancos al Horno con Carne de Cerdo

Makes 8 servings

White beans, also called cannellini, have a nutty flavor.

3 cups dried white beans, cleaned and soaked overnight (page 18)
2 teaspoons dry mustard
1/4 cup cider vinegar
1 teaspoon ground ginger
1/2 cup dark brown sugar, packed
1 small onion, diced
1 cup chicken stock (page 52)
1/2 pound lean side pork (page 27)
2 large pork hocks

Preheat the oven to 275°F.

Drain the soaked beans in a strainer and rinse them lightly with cold running water. Place the beans in a medium-size casserole dish. Add the mustard, vinegar, ginger, brown sugar, onion, and chicken stock, and mix together.

With a sharp paring knife, trim off any tough outer skin on the side pork and pork hocks. Add to the casserole, placing the side pork in the center with a hock on each side. Cover and bake for 6 hours. Beans should have absorbed most of the liquid and the sauce will be thick. Serve hot, cutting a little piece of the meat off the bone for each serving.

TRI-COLORED BEAN SALAD WITH BACON DRESSING
Ensalada de Frijoles de Tres Colores con Aliño de Tocineta

Makes 6–8 servings

This colorful bean medley is a feast for the eyes as well as the palate. Soak the red beans and black beans separately so they will retain their distinctive colors.

10 cups water
½ cup dried black beans, cleaned and soaked overnight (page 18)
½ cup dried red kidney beans, cleaned and soaked over-night (page 18)

2 cups string beans, trimmed
5 strips bacon
½ cup vegetable oil
¼ cup white wine vinegar
2 tablespoons honey
Salt and freshly ground black pepper to taste.

In two medium-size pots, bring 6 cups of the water (3 cups in each) to a boil over high heat. Drain the soaked black and red beans separately in a strainer and rinse them lightly under cold running water. Add the black beans to one pot and the red beans to the other pot, reduce the heat to medium, and simmer for 45 minutes, until the beans are tender but not soft. Drain the beans in a colander and set aside to cool.

Cut the string beans in half. Bring the remaining 4 cups water to a boil in the bean pot. Add the string beans and cook 10 minutes. Drain the water, then quickly place the green beans in a bowl of ice water so they retain their color.

In a medium-size skillet, cook the bacon strips over medium heat until crispy. Measure 1 tablespoon of the bacon grease into a measuring cup and reserve.

Place all the beans in a large bowl and crumble the bacon over them. Add the vegetable oil to the bacon grease in the measuring cup, to equal ½ cup. In a small bowl, mix the oil and bacon grease, vinegar, honey, and salt and pepper. Pour over the beans, toss together, and serve warm.

CHILLED LENTIL SALAD WITH SPICY VINAIGRETTE
Ensalada Fría de Lentejas a la Vinagreta

Makes 8–10 servings

Lentils are one of the most ancient cultivated legumes, dating back to the seventh century A.D. They are highly nutritious, being composed of 25 percent protein, and are rich in iron and vitamin B. Lentils cook relatively easily, but must be watched carefully because they soften easily and can lose their texture and shape.

8 cups water
2 tablespoons salt
1 pound dried lentils, cleaned
  (page 18)
¼ cup olive oil
¼ cup white wine vinegar

½ teaspoon dried ground cumin
½ teaspoon dried ground
  coriander
1 teaspoon cayenne pepper
1 teaspoon salt

In a large pot, bring the water and salt to a boil. Add the lentils, reduce the heat to medium-low, and cook for 30 minutes or until the lentils are tender but not overcooked. Drain.

In a colander, rinse the cooked lentils under cold water until slightly cool, then place them in a large ceramic mixing bowl. Mix the lentils together with the oil, vinegar, cumin, coriander, cayenne, and salt. When well combined, chill in the refrigerator for 1 to 2 hours. Serve cold.

HONEY-RUM-BAKED BLACK BEANS
Frijoles Negros con Ron y Miel al Horno

Makes 4–6 servings

This dish takes quite a while to bake, but it is worth the wait. The interplay of hot and sweet spices makes it an exciting tropical variation of traditional black beans. It can be a delicious meal when served with warm buttered cornbread (see Breads chapter) and salad greens in a light vinaigrette.

12 strips bacon
2 large onions, finely chopped
1 garlic clove, minced
1¾ cups chicken stock (page 52)
1½ cups cider vinegar
1-inch piece fresh ginger root, chopped, or 1 teaspoon ground ginger
½ teaspoon freshly ground black pepper
1 tablespoon dry mustard
½ cup honey
¼ cup dark brown sugar, packed
¼ teaspoon ground cloves
¼ teaspoon ground cinnamon
1 pound dried black beans, cleaned and soaked overnight (page 18)
4 cups water
½ cup dark rum

In a large heavy pan, fry the bacon over medium-high heat until crisp. Drain on paper towels and set aside to cool. Discard all but 2 tablespoons of the bacon grease. In the remaining grease, sauté the onions and garlic over medium heat for 4 to 6 minutes, until translucent.

Add the chicken stock, vinegar, ginger, pepper, mustard, honey, brown sugar, cloves, and cinnamon to the pan. Stir well, while bringing to a boil over medium-high heat. Drain the soaked beans in a strainer and rinse them lightly under cold running water. Add the water and the beans to the stock. Stir until the liquid comes to a boil, then turn down the heat to low, cover, and simmer 1 hour, until the beans are tender.

Preheat the oven to 275°F.

Transfer the beans to a large bean pot or earthenware casserole with a lid. Stir in the rum, cover, and bake for 6½ to 7 hours.

Uncover and bake 30 minutes longer, to absorb the remaining liquid and form a slight soft crust on top. Check the crust carefully, since the black color of the beans makes it difficult to see them browning. When a crust has formed, remove the beans from the oven and serve hot.

BLACK BEAN FLAN
Flan de Frijoles Negros

Makes 6 servings

This recipe combines two Cuban favorites, black beans and flan, to create a luscious side dish that can be served either hot or cold.

1½ cups cooked black beans
  (page 96)
1 egg
1 cup milk
½ teaspoon salt

Dash of Tabasco sauce
2–4 tablespoons butter for greasing pan and muffin tin
Sprigs of fresh parsley, cilantro, or watercress for garnish

Preheat the oven to 350°F. In a small mixing bowl, measure ½ cup of the black beans and mash with the back side of a fork. Add the egg, milk, salt, and Tabasco. Mix together with a fork until smooth, with only lumps of bean skin showing. Add the whole beans and mix together gently until just blended.

Melt the butter in a small pan. With a pastry brush, use the butter to lightly grease a 6-compartment muffin tin (grease only 6 compartments if the tin holds more).

In a large roasting pan, place 1 inch of water. Fill the muffin compartments with the bean mixture, being sure to add enough whole beans (which settle to the bottom of the mixture) to each compartment. Place the muffin tin in the roasting pan and bake for 35 minutes.

Remove from the oven and let cool slightly. Run a small, thin paring knife around the outside rim of each flan. Place a cookie sheet on top of the muffin tin and turn upside down. Do not lift up muffin tin until you carefully tap each compartment to make sure each flan is out of the tin.

Let cool, or serve immediately, using a spatula to transfer the flan to individual serving plates. Garnish with sprigs of parsley, cilantro, or watercress alongside.

BLACK BEAN CHILI
Sopón de Frijoles Negros con Ají Picante

Makes 8 servings

This is a highly practical recipe to prepare ahead of time, since the flavor of the chili improves if you let it stand overnight and reheat it just before serving. It is an appetizing, substantial dish to offer to friends along with a full-bodied red wine and cornbread (Breads chapter) or Cuban Bread (page 218).

2 cups dried black beans, cleaned and soaked overnight (page 18)
6 cups water
1 medium green bell pepper, seeded, deribbed, and chopped
2 medium onions, chopped
1 tablespoon minced garlic
2 celery stalks, chopped
2 carrots, peeled and chopped
1/2 teaspoon cayenne pepper, or more to taste

3 cups peeled and seeded tomatoes
1 cup beer
1/4 cup white wine vinegar
1 pound ground beef, browned and drained of fat
1 pound smoked link sausage or chorizo, browned, drained of fat, and cut into 1/2-inch pieces
Chopped fresh parsley and scallion for garnish

Drain the soaked beans in a strainer and rinse them lightly under cold running water. In a large pot, bring the beans and water to a boil over medium-high heat. Stir in the green pepper, onions, garlic, celery, carrots, cayenne pepper, tomatoes, beer, and vinegar. Cover, reduce the heat to medium-low, and simmer 1 hour, or until the beans are tender. Add the beef and sausage and simmer for 1/2 hour.

Sprinkle with chopped parsley and scallions and serve immediately, or let cool at room temperature and then refrigerate overnight. Reheat by bringing to a simmer in a large pot. Garnish before serving.

MOLD OF YELLOW RICE WITH SHRIMP, SCALLOPS, AND RED PEPPER
Arroz Amarillo en Molde con Camarones, Vieiras y Ajíes Rojos

Makes 6–8 servings

This is the type of elegant side dish that might have been served to guests in a luxurious Havana hotel restaurant when Cuba was a prime tourist spot. The interplay of spices and seafood lends a sophisticated flavor.

3 cups fish stock (page 51)
2¼ cups white wine
½ pound scallops, rinsed and drained (and cut into bite-size pieces if using large sea scallops)
1 pound medium raw shrimp, in shells
2 cups long-grain white rice
¼ cup olive oil
1 red bell pepper, seeded, deribbed, and chopped (with a few slices julienned for garnish)

4 shallots, chopped
1 tablespoon chopped or pressed garlic
¼ cup chopped fresh basil (1 teaspoon dried basil may be substituted)
½ teaspoon ground saffron
Fresh basil leaves or parsley sprigs for garnish

Preheat the oven to 400°F. In a large saucepan, bring the fish stock and wine to a boil over high heat. Reduce the heat to medium, add the scallops, cover, and poach for 3 minutes. (The scallops will be slightly underdone, but will continue to cook once removed from the pan.) Remove scallops with a slotted spoon and set aside. Bring the stock back to a boil, add the shrimp to the pan, cover, and cook 4 minutes. Remove the shrimp and set aside to cool. Bring the stock back to boil, add the rice, cover, and reduce the heat to medium-low. Stirring occasionally, simmer 15 to 20 minutes, until the rice is tender and most of liquid is absorbed.

Meanwhile, heat the oil in a medium-size skillet. Sauté the bell pepper and shallots over medium heat for 4 to 6 minutes, until the shallots are translucent. Add the garlic, chopped basil, and saffron and stir together, then remove from the heat.

Peel and devein the shrimp (page 27). When the rice is done, mix the rice, scallops, shrimp, pepper, and shallots in a medium-size bowl. Press the mixture firmly into a 6-cup mold, preferably a ring-shaped mold with a nonstick or lightly oiled surface. Bake 10 minutes.

Unmold onto a large serving platter by placing the serving platter on top of the mold, then turning them upside down. Garnish with julienne slices of red bell pepper and basil leaves or parsley sprigs.

BEEF

The Spaniards began import-
ing cattle from Spain to Cuba soon after they began their
colonization of the island in the early sixteenth century. The
livestock flourished in the fertile grazing land of Cuba's rolling plains and soon the island was not only supplying its own
meat needs, but also exporting beef.

During the colonial era, beef was enjoyed by wealthy families nearly every day, at lunch or dinner. Their slaves invented imaginative ways to serve the beef, combining Spanish
traditions and local products. Many of Cuba's best beef dishes
are clearly descendants of Spanish foods, but have a unique
character. For example, Cuba's famous Ropa Vieja (shredded
beef in a tangy tomato sauce) differs from the original Spanish version in that it uses tomatoes, peppers, and a seasoned
oil called achiote oil. Many of these Cuban adaptations were
later adopted in mainland Spain.

Today, Cuban cooking is still meat-oriented, and beef is in
great demand for both lunch and dinner. However, although
cattle are still raised in Cuba, and beef dishes are commonly
available in tourist hotels, meat shortages persist and there
are often long lines to buy beef. Cuban-Americans are luckier
in this regard, and are able to fully indulge their appetites for
succulent steaks and flavorsome chopped beef dishes.

Once you taste these delicious, robust recipes, you'll under-
stand why beef is such a popular element of Cuban cooking.

ROPA VIEJA

Makes 6 servings

This dish was originally introduced to Cuba by Spanish sailors and was commonly served by the Havana innkeepers who catered to seafaring folk. The name means "old clothes," because the flank steak is shredded until it resembles rags. It is served traditionally with white rice.

2½ pounds flank steak
1 carrot, peeled
1 small onion, peeled
1 celery stalk
2 tablespoons Achiote Oil (page 120) or olive oil
1 large onion, finely diced
2 garlic cloves, minced or pressed
1 green bell pepper, seeded, deribbed, and chopped

3 canned mild green chilies, seeded and chopped (hot or extra-hot green chilies, if you prefer)
4 large ripe tomatoes, peeled, seeded, and chopped
2 tablespoons tomato paste
Dash of cayenne pepper, or more to taste

In a large pot, place the flank steak with enough water to cover. Add the carrot, the small onion, and the celery stalk. Bring to a boil, then reduce the heat to medium-low and simmer approximately 1½ hours, covered, until the meat is tender.

Remove from the heat and cool in the liquid. When cool enough to handle, remove the steak from the pot with a slotted spoon or spatula and place in a large bowl (reserving the stock in the pot). Using your hands, shred the beef into strings and set aside.

In a large frying pan, heat the oil over medium heat. Sauté the diced onions, garlic, and green pepper for 4 to 6 minutes, until the onion is translucent. Add the green chilies, tomatoes, tomato paste, and 2 cups of the reserved stock, and mix well. Add the cayenne pepper, cover, and simmer 15 to 20 minutes. Remove the lid and raise the heat to medium-high. Stir approximately 5 minutes, until the sauce has reached the desired consistency. Pour the sauce over the beef, toss and serve immediately.

ACHIOTE OIL
Aceite de Achiote

Makes 2 cups oil

Achiote oil is a bright orange-red oil used in Cuban cooking. It adds a unique flavor to Ropa Vieja (page 119), Picadillo (page 121), and Sofrito Sauce (page 185) and others. It is a seasoned oil made with achiote seeds (also called annato seeds), which come from red-flowered tropical trees. These seeds are surrounded by an orange-red pulp, which gives the oil its vivid coloring, adding a dark red color to food. The oil will keep in the refrigerator for several months. You can buy these seeds at Hispanic markets.

2 cups olive oil
½ cup achiote seeds

In a small saucepan, heat the oil over low heat. Add the seeds and cook about 5 minutes, stirring occasionally, until a rich orange color is obtained. Remove the oil from the heat and let cool.

Strain the oil through a sieve into a small jar and discard the seeds. Use the oil in another recipe, or store it in the refrigerator for later use.

PICADILLO

Makes 6 servings

Picadillo, a spicy version of chopped beef hash, is one of Cuba's most popular dishes. Traditionally, fried plantains and black beans and rice are served with it and each portion is topped with deep-fried eggs (eggs that have been fried by immersing in 375°–425° oil until firm). You can present your Picadillo in this manner or with lighter accompaniments such as cornbread and tossed greens.

¼ cup Achiote Oil (page 120) (olive oil may be substituted)
1 large onion, diced
1 large green bell pepper, seeded, deribbed, and finely chopped
2 garlic cloves, minced or pressed
½ teaspoon cayenne pepper
2 pounds ground lean beef
3 tomatoes, peeled, seeded, and chopped (approximately 2½ cups)
½ teaspoon ground cumin
2 tablespoons capers
Salt and freshly ground black pepper to taste

In a large skillet, heat the oil over medium-high heat. Add the onion, green pepper, garlic, and cayenne pepper. Sauté about 5 minutes, until the onions are softened, then add the beef. Break up the meat into small pieces while you stir the ingredients. Cook 8 to 10 minutes, until the meat is lightly browned and cooked through.

Add the tomatoes and cumin, cover, and reduce the heat to medium-low. Simmer for 15 minutes, then add the capers and simmer 5 minutes longer. Add salt and pepper to taste, and serve hot.

OXTAIL STEW
Rabo Encendido

Makes 4–6 servings

This stew is an old-fashioned Cuban favorite. The marrow inside the bones of the oxtail, coupled with the heavy seasonings, gives it a bold flavor. When you purchase the oxtail, ask your butcher to cut it into 2-inch pieces. Traditionally served with white rice.

5 pounds oxtail, cut into 2-inch
    pieces
1 cup flour
¼ cup olive oil
1 cup beef stock (page 54)
1 cup red wine
3 tablespoons tomato paste, mixed
    with 2 cups water
1 bay leaf

½ teaspoon dried thyme
¼ teaspoon ground allspice
¼ teaspoon grated nutmeg
2 onions, chopped
2 green bell peppers, seeded,
    deribbed, and coarsely chopped
2 cloves garlic, minced
Chopped fresh parsley and parsley sprigs for garnish

Trim any excess fat from the oxtails. Dredge the oxtails in the flour. Heat the oil in a large, deep pot over medium-high heat and brown the oxtails in it, approximately 2 minutes on each side.

Add the stock, wine, tomato paste mixture, bay leaf, thyme, allspice, nutmeg, onions, green pepper, and garlic. Bring to a boil, then cover, reduce the heat to low, and simmer 2 hours, stirring occasionally. While simmering, add more water as necessary.

Transfer the oxtail stew to a serving platter, garnish with parsley, and serve hot.

PALOMILLA STEAK
Bistec de Palomilla

Makes 6 servings

The sauce for this thin cut of top sirloin is prepared in the same skillet as the steaks to retain the brown juices. You will need to prepare this recipe in two batches unless you have two large skillets.

3 tablespoons butter
1 tablespoon olive oil
6 thin-sliced boneless sirloin steaks
  (less than ½ inch thick)

2 tablespoons fresh lemon juice
Salt and freshly ground black
  pepper to taste

In a large skillet, melt ½ tablespoon of the butter with ½ tablespoon of the oil over high heat. Continuously swirl the skillet until the butter foams and then the foam begins to subside. Place 3 of the steaks, with at least ½ inch between each one, in the skillet and sauté 1 minute on each side. Remove the steaks to a serving platter and keep warm in the oven while repeating the process with the remaining steaks.

Remove the steaks from the oven and place the remaining steaks on the serving platter. Drain excess grease from pan and discard. Add the lemon juice and salt and pepper and stir over medium heat, scraping up any brown bits. Add remaining two tablespoons butter and whisk until melted, then pour it over the steaks and serve.

BAKED YUCA STUFFED
WITH SHREDDED BEEF
Yuca al Horno con Carne de Res Desmenuzada

Makes 6 servings

This recipe is an example of how the Spanish settlers used vegetables native to Cuba to create imaginative meat dishes. The baked yuca dough holds in moisture as well as flavor when the beef is cooked.

2 quarts water
1 pound flank steak
2 pounds yuca, peeled and cut
   into ½-inch pieces (page 27)
¼ cup butter
2 eggs, beaten
1 teaspoon salt
1½ cups flour
2 tablespoons olive oil

1 large onion, finely chopped
4 cloves garlic, chopped
1 green bell pepper, seeded,
   deribbed, and finely chopped
5 large ripe tomatoes, peeled,
   seeded, and chopped
1 tablespoon cider vinegar
1 egg, beaten with 1 teaspoon
   water, for glaze

In a large soup pot, bring the water to a boil over high heat. Add the meat, reduce the heat to low, and simmer 2 hours. Using tongs, remove the meat to a platter and set aside to cool. Reserve the cooking liquid for another use.

Meanwhile, in a large saucepan over low heat, simmer the yuca with enough water to cover for approximately 50 minutes, until tender but still intact. Drain the yuca through a strainer, then transfer to a large mixing bowl and mash with the butter until the butter is melted. Slowly add the 2 beaten eggs while continuing to mash until the mixture is well blended and smooth. Add the salt and slowly add flour. Mix together until the mixture holds the shape of a ball when formed. Cover the bowl with plastic wrap and set aside.

Preheat the oven to 350°F. When the meat is cool enough to handle, shred the beef with your hands into strings. Heat the oil in a large sauté pan over medium heat. When hot, add the onion, garlic, and green pepper. When the onion is soft (approximately 5 minutes), add the tomatoes and vinegar. Sauté until most of the liquid has evaporated, then stir in the shredded beef. Remove the pan from the heat and set aside.

Place the dough on a lightly floured piece of wax paper and roll it out with a rolling pin to form a square about ¼ inch thick. Spread the beef filling evenly over the dough. Starting at one end, roll up the dough (lift the wax paper to assist rolling if necessary).

Place the roll on a lightly oiled baking pan and brush the dough lightly with the egg and water mixture. Bake on the middle rack of the oven for 1 hour. Carefully slice the meat roll into 6 pieces with a serrated knife. Transfer to plates with a spatula, and serve.

CUBAN POT ROAST
Boliche Asado

Makes 6–8 servings

This pot roast is marinated with lemon juice to make it extra juicy. It is then cooked as a one-pot meal with the vegetables, allowing all the assorted flavors to marry.

Juice from 1 lemon
1 teaspoon dried thyme
2 tablespoons chopped fresh cilantro
2 garlic cloves, minced
3 pounds chuck roast
2 tablespoons flour
2 tablespoons butter
2 tablespoons olive oil

1 red bell pepper, seeded, deribbed, and chopped
1 green bell pepper, seeded, deribbed, and chopped
2 cups beef stock (page 54)
1 cup water
8 small potatoes, peeled
2 onions, quartered

Mix together the lemon juice, thyme, cilantro, and garlic. Rub the roast with the herb mixture. Place in a large pan and cover with plastic wrap. Allow to marinate in the refrigerator for at least 1 hour.

Remove the roast and sprinkle evenly with the flour. In a large pot, melt the butter with the olive oil over medium-high heat. Add the roast and brown on all sides. Add the chopped red and green peppers and sauté for 2 to 3 minutes. Remove the peppers and set aside. Add the beef stock and water, bring to a boil over high heat, then cover, reduce the heat to medium, and simmer 2 hours.

Add the peppers, potatoes, and onions and simmer 45 minutes to 1 hour, until the potatoes are tender. Serve hot.

TAMALE PIE WITH SWEET AND SPICY MEAT FILLING
Tamal con Relleno de Carne Agridulce

Makes 6 servings

Mouth-watering tamale pies are a Spanish specialty. This Cuban version makes a delicious meal when served hot with tossed greens in a light vinaigrette on the side.

FILLING:

1 pound lean ground beef
1 large onion, chopped
1/4 cup chopped raisins
1/4 cup chopped roasted red peppers (page 25)
2 tablespoons capers

1 teaspoon light brown sugar
1 cup beef stock (see page 54)
1/2 teaspoon salt
1 teaspoon chili powder
1/4 teaspoon freshly ground black pepper

TOPPING:

3/4 cup cornmeal
1 tablespoon flour
1/2 teaspoon salt
1 tablespoon sugar
1/2 teaspoon baking powder

1 egg, slightly beaten
1/4 cup chopped mild canned green chilies
1/3 cup milk
1 tablespoon olive oil

Preheat the oven to 350°F. In a large skillet, brown the meat over medium heat. Add the onion, raisins, roasted peppers, capers, brown sugar, beef stock, salt, chili powder, and pepper. Cover and let simmer 15 minutes. Uncover and simmer 5 minutes more. Place the meat filling in a lightly greased 2-quart casserole and set aside while making the topping.

In a large bowl, mix together the cornmeal, flour, salt, sugar, and baking powder. Stir in the egg, green chilies, milk, and oil. Evenly spread the cornmeal topping over the meat mixture. (The topping may sink a little into the filling, but it will rise when cooking.)

Bake 25 minutes, or until the topping is lightly browned. Serve hot.

SPICY STUFFED PEPPERS WITH TOMATO SAUCE
Ajíes Picantes Rellenos con Salsa de Tomate

Makes 6 servings

As is typical of Cuban cooking, mild green chilies are used in the stuffing for this recipe, not hot chilies, so the dish is spicy without being fiery. If you like your green bell peppers soft, you can pan-broil them or steam them for 2 to 3 minutes before filling; however, I prefer firmer peppers and do not precook them. Serve these peppers with steaming white rice.

STUFFED PEPPERS:

2 tablespoons butter
½ teaspoon ground cumin
1 garlic clove, minced
1 medium onion, chopped
1 pound lean ground beef
¼ cup minced mild canned green chili peppers

1 cup cooked long-grain white rice (page 95)
6 large green bell peppers, cut lengthwise, then seeded and deribbed

TOMATO SAUCE:

2 tablespoons butter
2 tablespoons olive oil
1 garlic clove, minced
3 cups peeled and seeded tomatoes
1 tablespoon light brown sugar

1 tablespoon malt or cider vinegar
¼ cup minced fresh cilantro
Salt and freshly ground black pepper to taste

Preheat the oven to 350°F. In a sauté pan, melt the butter over medium heat. Add the cumin, garlic, and onion and sauté 4 to 6 minutes. Add the meat and sauté 8 to 10 minutes, until cooked through, breaking up any large pieces as you cook.

Drain any excess grease from the pan and put the meat mixture into a mixing bowl. Stir in the green chilies and rice. Fill the peppers with the mixture. Arrange the peppers in a lightly greased roasting pan and set aside while making the sauce.

In a medium-size saucepan, melt the butter with the olive oil over medium heat. Add the garlic and sauté approximately 3 minutes, until tender. Add the tomatoes, brown sugar, vinegar, and cilantro, and salt and pepper to taste. Simmer 10 minutes, uncovered.

Pour the sauce over the peppers and bake 20 minutes. Serve hot.

MEAT-AND-ONION-STUFFED TURNOVERS
Empanadillas de Carne y Cebolla

Makes 12 turnovers

These tasty Cuban turnovers are ideal finger foods to serve to guests as appetizers, since they can be prepared ahead of time. They are typical of the snacks that street vendors sell during Carnival in Cuba and Miami.

FILLING:

1 pound lean ground beef
1 onion, diced
1 garlic clove, minced or pressed
½ teaspoon cayenne pepper

Salt and freshly ground black
*   pepper to taste*
2 tablespoons olive oil

DOUGH:

2 cups flour
1 teaspoon baking powder
1 teaspoon salt
½ cup butter, chilled and cut
*   into bits*

¼ cup cold water
1 egg, beaten with 1 teaspoon
*   water, for pastry glaze*

In a large mixing bowl, combine all the filling ingredients except the oil. Sauté the mixture in olive oil in a large frying pan over medium-high heat for 6 to 8 minutes, until the meat is browned. Cover and set aside while making the dough.

In a large mixing bowl, combine the flour, baking powder, and salt. Using your fingers or a fork, form a well in the center of the flour mixture. Using a pastry blender, a fork, or your fingers, cut (blend) the butter into the flour mixture until it resembles a coarse meal. Sprinkle the dough with the water and toss lightly until it just holds together, then form it into a ball. Wrap it in wax paper or plastic wrap and chill in the refrigerator 1 hour.

Preheat the oven to 400°F. When the dough is chilled, roll it out on a lightly floured surface. Roll it as thin as possible (approximately ⅛ inch thick). Cut out 12 4-inch-wide squares. Place 1 heaping tablespoon of filling in the center of each square and fold the dough over diagonally, forming a small triangle. Lightly press the edges together, moistening with a little water if necessary to seal the edges. Brush the tops of the turnovers with the beaten egg.

Place the turnovers on an ungreased cookie sheet and bake for 30 minutes. Remove from the oven and serve warm.

PASTELES

Makes 16 pasteles

Pasteles are steamed meat patties that are served as appetizers at Christmas dinners and are also presented to carolers and neighboring children. This tradition began in Puerto Rico and then became popular in Cuba. These savory little Christmas packages are traditionally steamed in banana or plantain leaves, but for the sake of expediency, this recipe substitutes kitchen parchment paper.

FILLING:

½ pound lean ground beef
½ pound lean ground pork
½ pound chopped ham
1 onion, chopped
2 garlic cloves, chopped
½ cup chopped, seeded, and
   deribbed green bell pepper

¼ cup chopped fresh cilantro
1 tablespoon capers
2 tomatoes, peeled, seeded, and
   chopped
½ teaspoon cayenne pepper
½ teaspoon salt

DOUGH:

Parchment paper
Butter or olive oil to lightly grease
   parchment paper
½ cup cornmeal
½ cup flour

½ teaspoon baking powder
½ teaspoon salt
3 tablespoons butter, chilled and
   cut into bits
2–4 tablespoons cold water

In a large bowl, mix together all the filling ingredients. Set aside while making the dough.

Cut the parchment paper into 16 10-inch by 8-inch pieces. Grease the paper lightly with butter or olive oil.

In a large mixing bowl, mix together the cornmeal, flour, baking powder, and salt, then form a well in the center. Drop the butter into the center of the well, and with your fingertips quickly rub the meal and butter together until they resemble coarse flakes. Pour 2 tablespoons of the cold water over the mixture. Toss together lightly and gather the dough into a ball. If the dough seems crumbly, add up to 2 table-spoons more cold water, a teaspoon at a time, until the dough holds together without being sticky.

Divide the dough into 16 equal parts (by separating the dough in half and then the halves by half, and so on, until you have 16 pieces). Divide the filling into 16 equal portions.

Spread a piece of dough in the center of a piece of parchment paper, so it covers 4 to 5 inches. Top the dough with a portion of filling. Fold each outside end of paper toward middle to make a neat package. Repeat the process with the remaining dough. With kitchen string, tie the patties securely together in pairs, with the folded sides inside.

Fill a large pot halfway with water and bring to a boil over high heat. Lower the patties into the water, either on a rack or using a slotted spoon. Bring the water back to a boil, then cover and reduce the heat to medium. Simmer 45 minutes, turning the patties once during cooking.

Using a slotted spoon, remove the patties from water and drain on paper towels. When the patties are cool enough to handle but still hot, remove the string. Serve the patties in the parchment on individual warm serving plates.

FLANK STEAK WITH PORT WINE MARINADE
Bistec en Vino Dulce

Makes 4–6 servings

This succulent flank steak recipe is very versatile. After the steak has been marinated, you can either broil or grill it. For a formal dinner, you can serve it with black beans and white rice or yuca with bitter orange and avocado with vinaigrette.

2½ pounds flank steak

PORT WINE MARINADE:
Juice from 2 lemons *1 cup port wine*
Juice from 2 oranges *One 2-inch slice ginger root,*
¼ cup honey *grated*
¾ cup olive oil *4 garlic cloves, sliced*

Place the flank steak in a large glass dish. In a medium-size bowl, mix together all the marinade ingredients. Pour the marinade over the steak and marinate in the refrigerator at least 1 hour, or overnight.

When ready to cook, either light the charcoal grill or heat the oven to broil. Grill over hot coals approximately 3 to 4 minutes on each side, or broil in the broiling pan 3 to 4 minutes on each side or until just dark on the outside and still rare on the inside. Flank steak will be tough if not cooked rare and if not cut across the grain. Cut the steak in thin slices diagonally across the grain, and serve.

ROLLED STUFFED STEAK
Bistec en Rollo

Makes 4–6 servings

This zesty dish can be accompanied by Cuban root vegetables, such as mashed plantains or boniatos, or by white rice.

2½ pounds flank steak
½ teaspoon salt
Juice from 1 lemon
¼ teaspoon freshly ground black pepper
2 garlic cloves, minced
3 thin slices smoked ham
1 carrot, grated

1 small onion, diced
1 tablespoon light brown sugar
1 tablespoon butter, cut into bits
3 tablespoons olive oil
¼ cup dry red wine
1 bay leaf
1 cup peeled, seeded, and chopped tomatoes

Rub one side of the flank steak with salt, lemon juice, pepper, and garlic. Layer the ham on top of the steak, then spread the carrot and onion on top of the ham. Sprinkle with the brown sugar and dot with the butter. Roll the steak, going against the grain, and tie the ends and middle with kitchen string.

In a large pot, heat the olive oil over medium heat. Brown the steak on all sides. Add the wine, bay leaf, and tomatoes and simmer 2½ hours, until the meat is tender and the sauce has thickened. Slice the steak crosswise into ½-inch pieces and serve with the sauce ladled over the top. Serve while still warm.

PORK

Following the Spanish tradition, pork plays a major role in Cuban cooking. The Spanish colonizers imported pigs from the Old World to Cuba in the early sixteenth century and also brought along their love of pork dishes. Pork came to be Cuba's most popular meat, as well as the traditional fiesta food.

Cubans traditionally serve pork on Sundays and holidays, but it is also an everyday food. Cuban hero sandwiches consisting of pork, cheese, and ham are a lunchtime favorite, as is roast pork for dinner.

Pork is highly versatile: The fat can be used as cooking oil; the loin can be made into an elegant entrée; the shoulder makes a succulent roast; the chops are bursting with flavor. And almost any part of the pig can be cooked or made into sausage. There are many different ways to enjoy pork, and Cuban cooking incorporates the very best of them.

Pork requires thorough cooking to eliminate any trichinae or parasites that may be in the meat. The cooked meat should appear white or gray inside, not pink. I recommend using a meat thermometer. Although an internal temperature of 140°F. or 150°F. is now considered safe, you may want to stick to the older rule of 180°F. in order to feel absolutely certain. You may also check to see if the meat is done by piercing with a fork and then pressing lightly. If juices run clear, it is done; if they are pink it is not.

BRAISED LOIN OF PORK WITH PAPAYA
Pernil Asado con Papaya

Makes 6–8 servings

This is a spectacular dish when served on a large platter, resting on a bed of greens and topped with ripe papaya slices (watercress leaves for garnish).

6 slices side pork (page 27)
5 pounds pork loin
1 garlic clove, minced
1 medium onion, chopped
3 medium tomatoes, peeled and chopped
1 bay leaf
1 cup chicken stock (page 52)
1 cup water
1 cup papaya juice
1 ripe papaya, peeled and sliced (page 24)

In a large pot over medium heat, fry the side pork until lightly browned. Remove the side pork, drain on paper towels, and reserve. In the grease in the pot, lightly brown the pork loin over medium heat. Remove the pork to a platter and set aside.

Add the garlic, onion, tomatoes, and bay leaf to the pot. Sauté over medium heat for 2 minutes. Add the chicken stock, water, and papaya juice, and heat nearly to a boil, stirring constantly and scraping brown bits from the bottom of the pan. Just before the liquid boils, add the pork loin. Cover the pot and simmer approximately 1½ hours, turning every half hour or so, until the pork is tender. If the liquid gets too thick, add more water, ½ cup at a time. Strain sauce through a sieve.

When tender, remove the pork to a serving platter. Top with approximately ½ cup of sauce. Arrange the papaya slices around the pork. Crumble the reserved side pork and sprinkle over the top, then serve.

PORK TENDERLOIN SAUTÉED WITH BITTER ORANGE AND GARLIC
Lomo de Cerdo Sofrito con Naranja y Ajo

Makes 4 servings

The bitter orange juice adds a splash of tartness to this quick and easy, moist and tender pork dish.

1 tablespoon butter
1 tablespoon olive oil
4 cloves garlic, minced
3 pounds pork tenderloin,
    trimmed and cut into
    ½-inch-thick slices

1 tablespoon bitter orange juice
    (page 18)
Salt and freshly ground black
    pepper to taste

In a large skillet over medium-high heat, melt the butter with the oil. Add the garlic and sauté 1 minute. Add the pork and sauté 6 to 8 minutes on each side, until the meat is lightly browned, stirring frequently with a wooden spoon. Pour the bitter orange juice over the pork and stir. Add salt and pepper to taste, and serve.

BABY BACK RIBS
WITH SPICY PAPAYA SAUCE
Costillitas al Horno con Salsa Picante de Papaya

Makes 6 servings

Baby back ribs are especially tender and have less fat than beef ribs. Marinating the ribs overnight, or at least 6 hours, makes them delectably succulent.

2 cloves garlic
¼ cup tomato paste
½ cup honey
1 cup chopped papaya (page 24)

½ cup white wine
½ cup water
4–5 pounds baby back pork spareribs

In the workbowl of a food processor, place the garlic, tomato paste, honey, papaya, white wine, and water. Puree the mixture by pulsing until blended, about 15 seconds. Place the ribs in the bottom of a large glass or ceramic dish and pour the marinade over them. Cover with plastic wrap and marinate in the refrigerator overnight, or at least 6 hours.

Preheat the oven to 400°F. Remove the ribs from the marinade and place in a roasting pan. Bake on the middle rack of the oven for 1½ hours, basting every 15 minutes with marinade. Remove from the oven, transfer to a warm serving platter, and serve.

HOMEMADE SPANISH SAUSAGE
Chorizo

Makes 4 servings

Spain and Portugal are famous for their spicy sausages. Spanish sausage, called chorizo, is used in many Cuban dishes, and is also eaten plain as an appetizer or snack. These sausage patties can be served for lunch or dinner with rice or beans, or frozen until you need them for another recipe.

1 pound lean ground pork　　　*2 tablespoons ground cumin*
½ cup cider vinegar　　　　　*¼ cup chopped fresh cilantro*
1 teaspoon salt　　　　　　　*⅛ teaspoon cayenne pepper*
4 cloves garlic, minced

In a large mixing bowl, mix all the ingredients together. Blend thoroughly, then cover with plastic wrap and let sit in refrigerator overnight, or at least 6 hours.

Shape the sausage mixture into patties and fry in a large skillet over medium-high heat until crispy brown on the outside and cooked through on the inside, about 5 minutes on each side. Remove with a slotted spoon, and serve, use in another recipe, or freeze until needed.

CIDER-AND-MANGO-ROASTED HAM
Jamón Asado con Sidra y Mango

Makes 20 servings

This recipe is ideal for dinner parties, since it uses a 10-pound ham, which will serve 20 people easily. When served with black beans and rice, fried plantains, and a green vegetable or avocado in a light vinaigrette, it makes a fabulous tropical feast.

Half a smoked ham (approximately 10 pounds), preferably shank end
10–15 whole cloves
¾ cup dark brown sugar, packed
1 teaspoon dry mustard
½ cup tart apple cider
½ cup finely chopped fresh mango (page 23)
Greens and pineapple chunks for garnish (optional)

Preheat the oven to 425°F. Place the ham fat side up in a large roasting pan and roast uncovered for 1 hour.

Remove the ham from the oven and remove the rind (if any), being careful not to remove the fat. Using a sharp paring knife, score the fat diagonally, stroking left to right and then right to left, forming a diamond pattern on the surface of the ham. Insert the whole cloves into the centers of the diamond pattern.

In a small bowl, mix together the brown sugar, mustard, cider, and mango. Brush the glaze all over the ham. Return the ham to the oven and roast another hour, basting occasionally with the glaze. The meat temperature should be 180°F. when a meat thermometer is inserted.

Remove from the oven and serve on a large platter, lined with greens and pineapple chunks if desired.

ROAST PORK WITH PEPPERED BLACK BEAN SAUCE
Pernil Asado con Salsa de Frijoles Negros

Makes 8 servings

I have chosen a rib end of loin, but you may substitute other choice cuts, such as rib or shoulder, if you prefer.

A note of caution: Many people deglaze their roasting pans on top of a hot burner; however, this can warp pans. I recommend that you use a flat wooden spoon to scrape the pan drippings out of the roasting pan, then transfer the drippings to a large pan to make your gravy over the burner.

1 rib end of pork loin (5 pounds)
3 garlic cloves, minced
¼ cup chopped fresh cilantro
1 cup flour
1 teaspoon salt
½ teaspoon freshly ground black pepper
½ teaspoon cayenne pepper
½ teaspoon paprika
1 cup chicken stock (page 52)
½ cup cooked black beans (page 96)
5 crushed green peppercorns

Preheat the oven to 450°F. Rub the pork all over with the minced garlic and chopped cilantro, then set aside. In a large, deep platter, mix the flour, salt, black pepper, cayenne pepper, and paprika. Dredge the pork in the mixture, using your fingers to help sprinkle and pat the flour where needed. Reserve the remaining flour.

Place the pork fat side up in a roasting pan, place the pan in the oven, and reduce the heat to 350°F. Bake 2 hours, until the meat temperature reaches 180°F. when a meat thermometer is inserted (or juices run clear when pierced, not pink).

When the pork is done, remove from the oven, place on a serving platter, and set aside. Pour all but 2 tablespoons of the pan drippings from the roasting pan. Whisk in 1 tablespoon of the seasoned flour over medium heat. Add the chicken stock to the roasting pan and, using a flat wooden spoon, stir the stock and drippings together, scraping the bottom of pan.

Transfer the stock and drippings to a large pan. Add the black beans and peppercorns and whisk constantly for about 5 minutes, until you have reached the desired thickness. Pour the sauce over the pork, and serve hot.

SPICY HAM AND POTATO CROQUETTES
Jamón Picante y Croquetas de Papas

Makes 24 croquettes
(4 servings)

Croquettes are time-consuming, since they must be prepared, chilled, dredged, and then left to dry again before cooking. But it is well worth the effort to create these wonderful delicacies, which are crispy outside and lusciously soft inside.

If you have trouble with the balls or cones holding their shape while making croquettes, add small amounts of flour or potato. It also helps if you make sure that the ham you use is patted dry of any excess liquid before adding it to the recipe.

Croquettes are nice to serve as a side dish alongside a meat entrée or as an appetizer.

1 cup chopped smoked ham
3 cups mashed potatoes
2 eggs, beaten
½ teaspoon salt
½ teaspoon white pepper
½ teaspoon cayenne pepper
1 tablespoon chopped fresh chives
    (or 1 teaspoon dried chives)

2 eggs, slightly beaten
2 cups fine bread crumbs
Vegetable oil for frying
Papaya Chutney (page 41) for
    serving (optional)

In a large bowl, mix the ham, mashed potatoes, eggs, salt, white pepper, cayenne pepper, and chives. Cover, place in refrigerator, and chill about 2 hours. When chilled, shape into 24 little cones or balls.

Place the 2 slightly beaten eggs in a medium-size mixing bowl, and the bread crumbs in another bowl. Dip the croquettes in the eggs, then roll them in the bread crumbs, then place them on a rack to dry. Allow the croquettes to dry for 1 hour.

Fill a deep fryer with 2 to 3 inches of vegetable oil and heat to 375°F. Fry the croquettes, a few at a time, for 3 to 5 minutes, until golden brown. Remove with basket or slotted spoon. Drain on paper towels before serving. (If you do not have a deep fryer, fill a large skillet a third full with oil and heat over medium-high heat. Fry the croquettes a few at a time, turning so they brown evenly. Transfer to paper towels with a slotted spoon to drain.)

Serve hot, either plain or with Papaya Chutney on top.

PORK TAMALES
Tamales de Carne de Cerdo

Makes 16 tamales
Serves 3–4

In Cuba, banana leaves or corn husks are used as tamale wrappings. Banana leaves are hard to find in the States, but corn husks are available. You can husk ears of corn yourself and cook the kernels as a side dish, or buy dried corn husks at Hispanic markets. Dried corn husks need to be reconstituted with water before using.

32 corn husks (from approximately 20 ears of fresh corn)
Olive oil for greasing husks

FILLING:
1 pound ground pork
3 cloves garlic, minced
¼ cup minced mild canned green chilies
¼ cup minced roasted red peppers (page 25)

2 tablespoons malt or cider vinegar
1 tablespoon dark brown sugar
1 teaspoon salt
½ teaspoon freshly ground black pepper

DOUGH:
½ cup cornmeal
½ cup flour
½ teaspoon baking powder
½ teaspoon salt

3 tablespoons butter, chilled and cut into bits
2–4 tablespoons cold water

In a large mixing bowl, mix together all the filling ingredients. Set aside while making the dough.

Place the cornmeal, flour, baking powder, and salt in a large mixing bowl. Mix together, forming a well in the center. Drop the butter bits into the center of the well and, using your fingertips, quickly rub the cornmeal mixture and butter together until they form a coarse meal. Pour 2 tablespoons of the water over the mixture. Toss together lightly and gather the dough into a ball. If dough is crumbly, add up to 2 tablespoons more water, 1 teaspoon at a time, until the dough holds together without being sticky.

Divide the dough into 16 equal parts (by dividing it in half, then dividing the halves in half, and so on). Divide the filling into 16 equal portions.

Place 2 husks flat, with one leaf slightly overlapping the other by ¼ inch. Lightly grease the tops of the husks with olive oil. Place 1 portion of dough in the center of the corn husks, leaving ¼ inch around the perimeter. Place 1 portion of meat in the center of the dough. Repeat with the remaining husks, dough, and meat. Fold the corn husks around the meat and secure with kitchen string. Bring a large pot halfway full of water to a boil over high heat. Add the tamales, bring the water back to a boil, then cover and reduce the heat to medium-low. Simmer 45 minutes.

Remove the tamales with a slotted spoon and let drain on paper towels. When cool enough to handle, remove the string and serve the tamales in the corn husks.

PORK CHOPS IN WINE SAUCE
Chuletas en Salsa Vino

Makes 6 servings

If you serve this dish over steaming white rice, the rice will soak up the spirited wine sauce. You can conveniently prepare the rice while the pork chops are simmering.

1 cup flour
6 pork loin chops (approximately ½ pound each)
2 tablespoons olive oil
2 garlic cloves, minced
1 medium onion, diced

1 cup chicken stock (page 52)
½ cup white wine
2 tablespoons tomato paste
½ teaspoon freshly ground black pepper
Salt to taste

Place the flour in a large, deep plate. Dredge the pork chops in the flour and set aside.

Heat the olive oil in a large pot over medium-high heat. Add the pork chops and brown on each side. Add the garlic, onion, and chicken stock, and cover.

In a small mixing bowl or measuring cup, whisk together the wine and tomato paste with a fork until there are no lumps remaining. Add the mixture to the pot, reduce the heat to low, cover, and simmer gently for 1 hour.

Place the pork chops on a serving platter over a bed of white rice. Spoon sauce over the top, and serve.

FRIED PORK AND ONION PATTIES
Albóndigas de Carne de Cerdo con Cebolla

Makes 6 servings

Cuban-American children adore these sweet, savory, hamburger-shaped patties. In fact, these patties are so easy to make that even a child can prepare them. They make a low-cost but tasty dinner when served over white rice.

2 pounds lean ground pork
1 medium onion, diced
2 garlic cloves, minced
1 teaspoon salt
½ teaspoon freshly ground black pepper

1 teaspoon malt or cider vinegar
1 teaspoon sugar
½ teaspoon paprika
Olive oil to grease frying pan
2 tablespoons butter
1 large onion, thinly sliced

Preheat the oven to 200°F. In a large mixing bowl, mix together the ground pork, diced onion, garlic, salt, pepper, vinegar, sugar, and paprika. Form the mixture into small round patties, approximately 3 inches in diameter.

In a large, hot frying pan greased lightly with olive oil, fry the patties a few at a time over medium-high heat, until browned on the outside and cooked through (not red) on the inside. Remove the patties from pan and keep warm on a covered platter in the oven.

Drain the fat from the pan and melt the butter over medium heat. Sauté the onion slices until soft and lightly browned. Remove the platter from the oven, place the sautéed onions on top of the patties, and serve.

GRILLED GARLIC PORK
Carne de Cerdo a la Parrilla con Ajo

Makes 6–8 servings

This dish originated in Portugal, then spread to Cuba and other Caribbean islands via the Spanish colonizers. Traditionally the pork is deep-fried; however, I have found this robs it of some of its flavor and adds unnecessary calories, so I prefer to grill or broil the meat. In some island kitchens the pork is marinated for as long as 2 days before cooking, but 4 to 6 hours is long enough to saturate the pork with robust flavor. (Even though this recipe calls for a large amount of garlic, it will not be overpowering, since we blanch the garlic first to make the flavor more subtle.) This dish is perfect to serve with white rice (or another rice of choice from this book), rum-flavored black beans, and fried sweet plantains.

1 cup water
½ cup garlic cloves, peeled
1 sprig fresh thyme, chopped, or
    ½ teaspoon dried thyme
½ teaspoon cayenne pepper
2 teaspoons salt
Juice from 1 large lemon
¼ cup cider vinegar

½ cup olive oil
4 pounds boneless pork (tenderloin or loin roast), thinly sliced (approximately 1 inch thick, and pounded thinner between plastic wrap with meat pounder to approximately ¼ inch thickness)

In a small saucepan, bring the water to a boil and blanch the garlic for 4 minutes. Drain the water and chop the garlic. In a large ceramic or glass bowl, mix together the garlic, thyme, cayenne pepper, salt, lemon juice, vinegar, and oil.

Place the pork slices in the marinade and marinate in the refrigerator 4 to 6 hours. Remove the pork from the marinade and pat dry with paper towels.

If grilling, grill the meat over medium-hot coals for 3 to 4 minutes per side. If broiling, broil 2 inches from the heat source on a broiling pan for 3 to 4 minutes on each side. Serve hot.

CORNMEAL-AND-RAISIN-STUFFED PORK CHOPS
Chuletas Rellenas de Harina de Maíz y Pasas

Makes 6 servings

When buying pork chops, ask your butcher for loin chops with a bit of tenderloin included, as these are the choicest cuts. These succulent stuffed pork chops go well with string beans and yellow rice.

6 rib pork chops, 1 inch thick
3/4 cup soft bread crumbs
1/4 cup cornmeal
1/4 cup chopped onion
2 tablespoons chopped fresh parsley
2 celery stalks, chopped fine

1/4 cup chopped raisins
1/2 teaspoon salt
1–4 tablespoons milk
Dash of Tabasco sauce
1 teaspoon olive oil
3/4 cup water

Preheat the oven to 350°F. Lay each chop flat on a cutting board, slice from the meat side to the inside of the bone to form a pocket, then set aside.

In a large mixing bowl, combine the bread crumbs, cornmeal, onion, parsley, celery, raisins, and salt. Add the milk, 1 tablespoon at a time, until the stuffing is moistened but not wet. (The amount of milk you need depends on the dryness of the bread crumbs you use.) Add a dash of Tabasco sauce and mix well.

Fill each pork chop pocket with stuffing and close with skewers. (If skewers are unavailable, press the chops closed and transfer carefully to the skillet with a spatula.)

In a large skillet, heat the olive oil over medium heat. Add the pork chops, a couple at a time, and sear on each side, then place in a baking dish. Deglaze the skillet with the water and pour the liquid around the chops.

Cover the baking dish and bake the chops for 1 hour. Turn the heat up to broil, uncover, and baste the chops. Broil 4 to 5 inches from the heat source for 3 minutes, then serve.

HOT PEPPER PORK CHOPS
WITH CREAMY GRAVY
Chuletas en Su Salsa

Makes 6 servings

The creamy gravy adds a velvety richness to these juicy pork chops. This recipe would be well balanced by white rice to which a dash of parsley has been added for color.

½ cups flour
1 teaspoon salt
1 teaspoon paprika
½ teaspoon cayenne pepper
¼ teaspoon freshly ground black pepper

6 pork chops (½–¾ inch thick)
2 tablespoons olive oil
1 cup milk
Salt and freshly ground black pepper to taste

Preheat the oven to 200°F. In a large mixing bowl, combine the flour, salt, paprika, cayenne pepper, and black pepper. Dredge each pork chop in the mixture and set aside. Reserve remaining flour.

In a large skillet, heat the olive oil over medium-high heat. Add the pork chops and brown on each side. Reduce the heat to medium-low and cook 30 minutes uncovered. Remove the pork chops from the skillet, transfer to a large platter, and keep the uncovered platter warm in the oven while making the gravy.

Discard all but 2 tablespoons pan drippings from the skillet. Add 1 tablespoon of the reserved flour and whisk until smooth with a small whisk or fork over medium heat. Let cook 1 minute. Add the milk and whisk until the desired thickness is reached. Season with salt and pepper to taste.

Remove the pork chops from the oven, pour the gravy over them, and serve.

SWEET AND SOUR PAPAYA PORK
Carne de Cerdo Agridulce con Papaya

Makes 4 servings

An exotic blend of vibrant flavorings makes this an exciting Cuban-Chinese recipe for pork. It should be presented on a bed of white rice, which will absorb the sweet, spicy sauce.

8 pork chops (½ inch thick)
1½ cups flour
1½ teaspoons salt
1 teaspoon paprika
½ teaspoon ground ginger
¼ cup vegetable oil
½ cup pineapple juice
3 tablespoons butter
2 tablespoons brown sugar
1 teaspoon soy sauce

¼ cup malt vinegar
½ teaspoon grenadine
½ cup chicken stock (page 52), mixed with 1 teaspoon cornstarch
½ cup chopped papaya (page 24)
¼ cup chopped roasted red peppers (page 25)

Cut the fat from the pork chops, then cut the meat off bone and into 1-inch pieces. Place the flour, salt, paprika, and ginger in a large plastic bag and shake together. Place the pork in the bag and shake until all pieces are well coated. Remove the pork from the bag by hand, shaking each piece lightly to remove excess flour.

In a medium-size frying pan, heat the vegetable oil over medium-high heat. Brown the pork for 10 minutes, stirring so all the sides brown. Reduce the heat to medium-low, cover, and cook 20 minutes, until the pork is tender and cooked through.

Meanwhile, in a saucepan over medium-high heat, whisk together the pineapple juice, butter, brown sugar, soy sauce, vinegar, grenadine, and chicken stock mixture. Whisk continuously until the mixture thickens. Add the papaya and roasted red pepper, and stir well until heated thoroughly.

Transfer the pork to a large serving platter over a bed of white rice. Top with the sauce, and serve.

CUBAN-CHINESE ROAST LOIN OF PORK
Pernil Asado Estilo Chino-Cubano

Makes 6–8 servings

The Chinese laborers who flooded into Cuba in the mid-nineteenth century introduced many Oriental spices to the island. This recipe utilizes some of these seasonings, which are available in gourmet shops, Oriental markets, and some supermarkets in the United States.

1 4–5 pound pork loin
3 tablespoons soy sauce
3 tablespoons sherry
2 tablespoons hoisin sauce
¼ cup mashed cooked black beans (page 96)

2 tablespoons 5-spice powder
2 tablespoons minced garlic
3 tablespoons sugar
¼ cup honey, mixed with ¼ cup boiling water, for basting

Preheat the oven to 425°F. Rinse the pork loin and pat dry. Place on a rack in a roasting pan, and fill the bottom of the pan with 1 inch of water.

In a mixing bowl, combine the soy sauce, sherry, hoisin sauce, mashed black beans, 5-spice powder, garlic, and sugar. Mix well. Coat the pork loin with the mixture, rubbing the meat all over until the mixture is used up.

Roast the pork 15 minutes, then reduce the heat to 325°F. and cook 1 to 1½ hours, basting every 15 minutes with the honey and water mixture.

When the pork is thoroughly cooked (the inside temperature reaches 180°F. and the juices run clear, not pink), remove it from the oven, let cool slightly, transfer to a serving platter, and serve.

POULTRY

Like beef and pork, poultry was introduced to Cuba by the Spanish settlers in the early sixteenth century. Since chickens are relatively easy to raise and inexpensive, they became a dietary staple of the lower classes. Wealthy plantation owners and traders also ate chicken, although they showed a preference for pork and beef. Today, because of the growing concern over cholesterol, chicken is gaining in popularity in the Cuban-American community.

Cuban cooking includes a number of delicious chicken dishes that combine Spanish culinary traditions with Caribbean produce. Chicken and rice are a basic coupling in Cuban cooking and the dishes in this section are well complemented by steaming white long-grain rice.

CHICKEN AND RICE
Arroz con Pollo

Makes 6–8 servings

This classic recipe is one of the most commonly served dishes among Hispanic people throughout the world. Since all the ingredients go in one skillet, the rice absorbs the flavor of the chicken juices, vegetables, and seasonings. For a "soupier" version, see next recipe.

¼ cup olive oil
1 3-pound chicken, cut into 6–8
  serving pieces
1 large onion, diced
3 garlic cloves, minced
1 green bell pepper, seeded,
  deribbed, and chopped
1¼ cups peeled, seeded, and
  chopped tomatoes
½ teaspoon salt
¼ teaspoon freshly ground black
  pepper
¼ teaspoon cayenne pepper

1 bay leaf
½ teaspoon paprika
¼ teaspoon ground saffron
  (turmeric may be
  substituted)
2 cups water
1½ cups white wine
1 10-ounce package frozen green
  peas
2 cups long-grain white rice
Roasted red pepper strips for
  garnish (page 25)

In a large skillet, heat the oil over medium heat. Add the chicken parts and sauté a few at a time until lightly browned on all sides. Remove the chicken and set aside on paper towels.

Drain the excess fat, leaving 1 tablespoon in the skillet. Add the onion, garlic, and green pepper, and sauté 3 to 5 minutes, until the onion is translucent but not brown. Add the tomatoes, salt, black pepper, cayenne pepper, bay leaf, paprika, saffron, and water. Cover and bring to a boil. Add the chicken, cover, and simmer over medium-low heat for 30 minutes. Add the wine, peas, and rice. Stir well and simmer, covered, for 20 minutes more.

Transfer to a large serving platter, garnish with roasted red pepper strips, and serve hot.

CHICKEN AND RICE STEW
Asopao con Pollo

Makes 6–8 servings

In Cuba, *arroz con pollo*, chicken and rice, is served either "grainy" or "soupy," depending on personal preference. This dish, which is actually a Puerto Rican national dish, is much like the soupy *arroz con pollo* served in Cuban households for centuries. Often a small amount of grated cheese is added right before serving.

3 garlic cloves, minced
1 teaspoon fresh oregano leaves (or ½ teaspoon dried oregano)
1 teaspoon salt
1 3-pound chicken, cut into 6–8 serving pieces
3 tablespoons olive oil
1 medium onion, diced
1 green bell pepper, seeded, deribbed, and chopped
½ cup diced ham
1½ cups peeled, seeded, and chopped tomatoes
2 cups long-grain white rice

6 cups chicken stock (page 52)
¼ teaspoon freshly ground black pepper
1 teaspoon paprika
1 tablespoon capers
¼ cup minced roasted red peppers (page 25)
¼ cup grated sharp white cheese (optional) (such as sharp white Cheddar)
4–5 long strips of roasted red peppers for garnish (page 25)

With a mortar and pestle (or in a small ceramic bowl, using the back of a spoon), mash together the garlic, oregano, and salt, forming a thick paste. Pat the chicken dry with paper towels and rub the paste on the chicken.

In a large pot, heat the olive oil over medium heat. Add the onion and green pepper, and sauté until the onion is translucent but not brown. Add the ham and tomatoes, and sauté 3 to 5 minutes. Add the chicken, cover, reduce the heat to low, and simmer ½ hour. Using tongs, transfer the chicken to a plate and set aside to cool.

Stir the rice, chicken stock, black pepper, paprika, capers, and minced red peppers into the pot. Cover and cook over low heat for 20 minutes.

When cool enough to handle, remove the chicken meat from the bones and cut into bite-size pieces. When the rice mixture is finished cooking, stir in the chicken, cover, and cook 5 minutes longer. Taste, and add cheese if desired. Serve in bowls, garnished with roasted pepper strips.

BREAST OF CHICKEN AL AJILLO
Pechuga de Pollo al Ajillo

Makes 4 servings

"Al ajillo," or "with garlic sauce," is a popular way to prepare shrimp or chicken in Cuban kitchens. The use of parsley
in this recipe reflects the Portuguese influence on Cuban
cooking.

2 whole boneless, skinless chicken
    breasts (approximately 2
    pounds)
2 tablespoons olive oil
4 cloves garlic, thinly sliced

¼ cup white wine
2 tablespoons chopped fresh
    parsley
2 tablespoons chopped fresh
    cilantro

Cut the chicken breasts in half along the breastbone line and
set aside. Heat the olive oil in a large sauté pan over medium-
high heat. Add the chicken breasts and cook until browned,
approximately 2 minutes on each side. Add the garlic and
sauté 2 to 3 minutes. Add the white wine, parsley, and
cilantro. Cover, reduce the heat to medium, simmer 5 minutes, and serve.

SPICY CHICKEN SAUTÉ WITH VEGETABLES AND PAPAYA
Pollo Picante con Vegetales y Papaya

Makes 4–6 servings

Stir-frying vegetables is a technique that the Chinese laborers introduced to Cuba. This is a healthful and low-cholesterol dish with a lively flavor. Serve over steaming white rice.

2 tablespoons olive oil
1 large onion, diced
1 green bell pepper, seeded, deribbed, and coarsely chopped into ½-inch pieces
1 red bell pepper, seeded, deribbed, and coarsely chopped into ½-inch pieces
1 garlic clove, chopped
2 pounds boneless, skinless chicken breasts, cut into 1-inch cubes

1 teaspoon salt
1 teaspoon paprika
½ teaspoon cayenne pepper
¼ teaspoon freshly ground black pepper
¼ cup chopped fresh parsley
1 teaspoon malt or cider vinegar
¼ teaspoon ground cumin
¼ teaspoon ground ginger
¾ cup chopped papaya, cut into 1-inch pieces (page 24)

In a large sauté pan, heat 1 tablespoon of the olive oil over medium-high heat. Add the onion, green pepper, red pepper, and garlic and stir-fry for 3 to 4 minutes, until slightly tender and lightly browned. Remove with a slotted spoon and set aside.

Add the remaining tablespoon of olive oil to the pan. Add the chicken, salt, paprika, cayenne pepper, black pepper, parsley, vinegar, cumin, and ginger. Sauté until the chicken is cooked through and lightly browned. Add the vegetables and papaya, and continue to sauté for 3 minutes. Serve immediately.

COCONUT-STUFFED CHICKEN BREASTS WITH LIGHT CREAM SAUCE
Pechugas de Pollo Rellenas de Coco con Salsa de Crema

Makes 6 servings

The fresh coconut adds tropical allure to this succulent chicken dish. It is lovely when served on a bed of white rice, with the luxurious cream sauce poured over the top and green garnishes lining the platter.

STUFFED CHICKEN:

6 boneless and skinless chicken breast halves
Sprinkling of salt and freshly ground black pepper
1 teaspoon butter
¼ cup grated fresh coconut

¼ cup chopped fresh cilantro (parsley may be substituted)
Butter for greasing baking dish
¼ cup melted butter
¼ cup chicken stock (page 52)

CREAM SAUCE:

2 tablespoons butter
2 tablespoons flour
½ cup heavy cream
¼ cup chicken stock (page 52)

¼ cup white wine
Salt and freshly ground black pepper to taste

Preheat the oven to 350°F. Place the chicken breasts flat on the surface of a cutting board and pound lightly to make the chicken flatter and easier to roll. Sprinkle them lightly with salt and pepper. In a small sauté pan, melt the 1 teaspoon butter over medium heat. Add the coconut and cilantro, and sauté until cooked through, approximately 6 to 8 minutes.

Spread the coconut mixture on the chicken breasts, and roll them up lengthwise. Place the chicken breasts seam side down in a lightly greased baking dish. Brush each breast with the melted butter. Pour the chicken stock around the chicken and cover the dish with foil. Bake 35 to 45 minutes.

Meanwhile, make the sauce. In a medium-size saucepan,

melt the butter with the flour over low heat and cook 3 to 4 minutes while stirring. Slowly (so it does not become lumpy), whisk in the cream, then the chicken stock and wine. Cook over medium heat, whisking continuously, until the sauce has thickened to the desired texture, approximately 8 to 10 minutes.

Remove the chicken breasts from the oven and serve on a bed of white rice with the cream sauce spooned over the top.

COUNTRY BAKED CHICKEN
Pollo Dorado al Horno

Makes 6 servings

The small amount of sweet raisins with the hot seasoning in this recipe typifies the happy marriage of sweet and spicy flavors in Cuban cooking.

½ cup flour
1½ teaspoons salt
½ teaspoon freshly ground black
  pepper
1 teaspoon paprika
1 3-pound chicken, cut into
  6–8 serving pieces
¼ cup olive oil
2 onions, finely chopped
1 green bell pepper, seeded,
  deribbed, and finely chopped
1 red bell pepper, seeded,
  deribbed, and finely chopped
3 garlic cloves, minced

½ teaspoon cumin
¼ cup chopped fresh parsley
¼ cup chopped scallions
3 cups peeled, seeded, and
  chopped tomatoes
1 cup white wine
1 cup chicken stock (page 52)
2 cups cooked long-grain white
  rice (page 95)
Butter for greasing pan or dish
¼ cup chopped raisins
Chopped fresh parsley and parsley sprigs for garnish

Preheat the oven to 350°F. In a deep platter or small mixing bowl, mix the flour, 1 teaspoon of the salt, ¼ teaspoon of the pepper, and the paprika. Dredge the chicken pieces in the flour mixture and set aside.

In a large frying pan, heat the olive oil over medium heat. Sauté the chicken pieces, a few at a time, until lightly browned on all sides. Remove and drain on paper towels. Add the onions, green pepper, red pepper, garlic, and cumin and the remaining salt and black pepper to the pan. Sauté until the onions are translucent but not brown. Stir in the parsley, scallions, and tomatoes. Add the white wine and chicken stock. Remove from the heat and set aside.

Place the chicken in a lightly greased, shallow roasting pan or baking dish. Pour the tomato mixture over the chicken, cover the pan with foil, and bake 45 minutes. Meanwhile, prepare the rice. When the rice is finished, stir in the chopped raisins.

Place the rice on a large, warm serving platter. Place the chicken on top of the rice. Garnish with sprinkles of chopped fresh parsley on top and sprigs alongside before serving hot.

CHICKEN CROQUETTES WITH SAUTÉED ONIONS AND PEPPERS
Croquetas de Pollo con Sofrito de Cebollas y Ajíes

Makes 24 croquettes
(4 entrée servings)

These luscious chicken croquettes can be served as an entrée topped with sautéed onions and peppers as in this recipe or as an appetizer with Orange Cocktail Sauce without the onions and peppers (page 42). For additional hints on preparing croquettes, see the Spicy Ham and Potato Croquette recipe, page 148. When preparing the chicken stock for this recipe, do not add much salt, as the stock will be reduced during the cooking. I do not suggest using canned stock for this recipe, but if you substitute a canned broth, use a low-salt variety.

CROQUETTES:
2 tablespoons butter
3 tablespoons flour
2 cups unsalted chicken stock
  (page 52)
1½ cups minced cooked chicken
  (preferably white meat)

¼ cup minced fresh parsley
¼ teaspoon white pepper
2 eggs, beaten
2 cups fine bread crumbs
Vegetable oil for frying

ONIONS AND PEPPERS:
2 tablespoons butter
1 tablespoon olive oil
2 garlic cloves, minced
1 large onion, cut lengthwise
  and thinly sliced
1 large green bell pepper, seeded,
  deribbed, and thinly sliced

1 large red bell pepper, seeded,
  deribbed, and thinly sliced
½ teaspoon salt
¼ teaspoon freshly ground black
  pepper

In a heavy saucepan over medium heat, melt the butter with the flour, stirring until well blended. Add the chicken stock and cook over low heat for approximately 20 minutes, whisking frequently, until reduced by half.

Place the chicken, parsley, and white pepper in a large mixing bowl. Add ¾ cup of the chicken stock mixture and blend together. Let cool in the refrigerator, covered with plastic wrap, until chilled (at least 2 hours).

Remove the chicken mixture from the refrigerator and shape into 24 2-to-3-inch cylinders. Place the eggs in a small bowl and the bread crumbs in another. Roll the croquettes in the egg, then in the crumbs, then place on a rack to dry for at least 1 hour.

Fill a deep fryer with 2 to 3 inches of vegetable oil and heat to 375°F. Fry the croquettes 3 to 5 minutes, a few at a time, until golden brown. (If a deep fryer is unavailable, fill a large skillet a third full with oil and heat over medium-high heat. Fry the croquettes 3 minutes on each side, until golden brown.) Remove the croquettes with a slotted spoon and drain on paper towels.

In a large skillet, melt the butter with the olive oil over medium-high heat. Add the garlic, onion, green pepper, red pepper, salt, and black pepper, and sauté until soft and lightly browned. Place the croquettes on plates, top with the sautéed onions and peppers, and serve.

ROASTED CHICKEN
WITH PAPAYA GLAZE
Pollo Asado con Salsa de Papaya

Makes 4 servings

The papaya and orange juice turn this marinated chicken into a fruity tropical delight. This superb entrée will look as good as it tastes if you serve it on a large platter lined with watercress and parsley.

1 3½-pound roasting chicken
1 teaspoon salt
1 cup orange juice
¼ cup light brown sugar
2 shallots
1 bay leaf
1 tablespoon Dijon mustard
2 garlic cloves
1 ripe papaya, peeled and cut
    in half, with 1 half sliced
    thin and reserved for garnish
    (page 24)

¼ teaspoon dried thyme
½ teaspoon salt
¼ teaspoon freshly ground black
    pepper
1 tablespoon butter
Sprigs of fresh parsley and wa-
    tercress for garnish (optional)

Rub the chicken evenly with the salt, then set aside. In the workbowl of a food processor, combine the orange juice, brown sugar, and shallots. Pulse for 10 to 20 seconds, until the shallots are finely minced.

Place the chicken in a shallow dish and pour the orange juice mixture over it. Crumble the bay leaf over the chicken, then cover with plastic wrap. Marinate in the refrigerator for at least 6 hours, or overnight.

Preheat the oven to 375°F. Transfer the chicken to a roasting pan (reserving the marinade) and roast for a total of 1 hour and 45 minutes.

After putting the chicken in the oven, prepare the papaya glaze. Strain the marinade through a fine sieve into the workbowl of a food processor. Add the mustard, garlic, papaya half, thyme, salt, and black pepper. Pulse 10 to 20 seconds, until well blended and any garlic lumps are gone. Divide the mixture in half, using one half for basting the chicken and the other half for the sauce.

Baste the chicken with papaya glaze at least once every half hour while roasting. When the chicken is cooked, place it on a large, warmed serving platter, and set aside.

Pour off all but 2 tablespoons of the pan drippings and discard. Place the remaining 2 tablespoons drippings (scraping the bottom of the roasting pan to loosen the bits) in a small saucepan and whisk in the butter over medium heat. Add the remaining half of the glaze to the saucepan and cook 4 to 5 minutes.

Pour some sauce over the chicken and place the reserved papaya slices on top. Place remaining sauce in serving dish, garnish the platter with parsley and watercress, if desired, and serve immediately.

ROASTED GAME HENS WITH BITTER ORANGE GLAZE
Gallinitas Asadas con Salsa de Naranja

Makes 4 servings

To make this elegant entrée, you use either fresh bitter oranges (also called Seville oranges), which are available in Florida, or bottled bitter orange juice, which is sold at Hispanic markets throughout the country. You can use either fresh or frozen game hens in this recipe, although fresh are preferable. If you use frozen hens, allow them to thaw at least 4 to 6 hours before cooking.

Olive oil to lightly grease roasting
  pan
4 game hens (1½ pounds each)
1 onion, quartered
2 tablespoons chopped scallions
2 bitter oranges, or ¼ cup bottled bitter orange juice

¼ cup honey
¼ cup white wine
½ teaspoon dry mustard
2 tablespoons minced parsley
Sliced orange and chopped fresh
  parsley for garnish

Preheat the oven to 450°F. Place the hens in a lightly greased roasting pan, breast side up. Place 1 onion quarter in the cavity of each hen. Slipping your hand underneath the top layer of skin of the breast, separate the skin from the meat. Divide 1 tablespoon of the chopped scallions into 4 portions and distribute evenly under the skins of the hens. Set aside.

Squeeze the juice from the bitter oranges into or add the bottled bitter orange juice to a medium-size mixing bowl. Stir in the honey, wine, mustard, and parsley, and the remaining scallions. When well mixed, drizzle half of the mixture over the hens and reserve the other half for basting. Place the hens in the oven and reduce the heat to 350°F. Roast approximately 1½ hours, basting every 15 minutes with the reserved glaze and pan drippings. Garnish each hen with sliced oranges and parsley before serving.

SWEET AND SPICY CILANTRO CHICKEN
Pollo Agridulce con Cilantro

Makes 4–6 servings

This recipe offers a simple and low-fat, yet enticing way to prepare chicken. The blending of exotic spices gives it a flavor similar to curries, which are very popular in the West Indies. Serve over steaming white rice.

4 whole boneless, skinless chicken breasts
1 tablespoon olive oil
1 tablespoon butter
1 large onion, finely chopped
2 garlic cloves, minced
2 green apples (such as Granny Smith), peeled, cored, and chopped

1 tablespoon ground coriander
¼ cup chopped fresh cilantro
¼ teaspoon ground turmeric
½ teaspoon ground ginger
½ teaspoon salt
½ teaspoon ground cumin
Fresh cilantro sprigs for garnish

Cut the chicken breasts into bite-size pieces. In a large skillet, heat the olive oil with the butter over medium heat. Add the chicken and sauté until lightly browned. Add the onion, garlic, apple, coriander, cilantro, turmeric, ginger, salt, and cumin. Cover and simmer 10 minutes over medium-low heat. Stir well and serve garnished with fresh cilantro sprigs.

GOLDEN BAKED CHICKEN WITH TOMATOES, OLIVES, AND CAPERS
Pollo Dorado al Horno con Tomates, Aceitunas, y Alcaparras

Makes 4–6 servings

Capers add sharpness and character to many Cuban dishes. When handling capers, always remove them from the jar with a small spoon, since touching the liquid in which they are immersed and then returning the capers to the refrigerator can cause them to become rancid. Serve this flavorful chicken over a bed of steaming white rice.

2 garlic cloves, minced
½ teaspoon dried thyme
3 tablespoons malt or cider vinegar
½ teaspoon salt
¼ teaspoon freshly ground black pepper
1 frying chicken (4 pounds), cut into 6–8 serving pieces
⅔ cup flour

2 tablespoons butter
3 tablespoons olive oil
½ cup white wine
2 large onions, thinly sliced
1 large tomato, peeled, seeded, and diced
¼ cup chopped black olives
1 tablespoon green capers
1 tablespoon chopped fresh parsley for garnish

Preheat the oven to 350°F. In a small bowl, combine the garlic, thyme, vinegar, salt, and pepper. Rub the mixture all over the chicken pieces. Place the flour in a shallow plate and dredge the chicken in it. In a large skillet, melt the butter with 1 tablespoon of the oil over medium heat. Lightly brown chicken on both sides in the skillet.

Transfer the chicken to a large casserole or baking dish. Pour the excess fat from the skillet and discard. Deglaze the pan by adding the white wine and cooking over high heat for 2 to 3 minutes while scraping the bottom of the skillet. Pour the wine around the chicken.

In the same skillet, heat 1 tablespoon of the oil over medium-high heat. Sauté the onions until lightly browned. Cover and simmer 3 to 5 minutes over medium heat, until the onions are tender. Uncover, raise the heat, and sauté until all the liquid has evaporated. Place the onions around the chicken.

In a small bowl, mix the diced tomato, olives, and capers with the remaining 1 tablespoon of olive oil. Combine well and sprinkle around the chicken.

Bake for 1 hour, or until tender. Serve garnished with sprinkles of chopped parsley.

CRISPY FRIED MARINATED CHICKEN
Pollo Frito al Escabeche

Makes 4 servings

The bitter orange marinade adds an unusual flavor to this fried chicken recipe, which is economical and simple to prepare.

2½ pounds boneless, skinless
   chicken breasts, cut into
   1–1½-inch cubes
5 garlic cloves, crushed
½ cup bitter orange juice (page
   18)

Vegetable oil for frying
1 cup flour
½ teaspoon freshly ground black
   pepper

Place the chicken in a glass dish, add the garlic cloves and bitter orange juice, and toss together. Cover the dish with plastic wrap and place in the refrigerator for ½ hour.

Remove the chicken from the refrigerator and drain the marinade. Fill a deep fryer a third full with vegetable oil and heat to 375°F. (or fill a large skillet a third full with oil and heat over medium-high heat).

Place the flour in a large, shallow dish and sprinkle with the pepper. Place a rack next to the dish. One piece at a time, dredge the chicken in the flour, making sure the entire surface is coated, then place on the rack to dry slightly while flouring the remaining chicken.

Deep-fry the chicken pieces a few at a time for 3 to 5 minutes in the fryer (or for 3 minutes on each side in a skillet). Place paper towels on the rack and drain the excess grease from the chicken after frying. Transfer to a large platter and serve.

GARLIC-MARINATED ROASTED CHICKEN
Pollo Asado al Ajillo

Makes 4–6 servings

The chicken sends an appealing aroma wafting through the kitchen while it's roasting, and when finished it's tender and juicy. You can prepare rice and beans and fried plantains to complete the dinner while the chicken is in the oven.

One 3-pound frying chicken,
*   cut in half*
10 garlic cloves, minced
¼ cup lime juice
1 teaspoon ground cumin
1 cup white wine

1 teaspoon salt
1 small onion
2 shallots
½ teaspoon freshly ground black
*   pepper*
¼ cup olive oil

Rub the chicken inside and out with the minced garlic. In the workbowl of a food processor, place all the remaining ingredients except the olive oil. Pulse 15 to 20 seconds, until the onion and shallots are liquefied.

Place the chicken in a glass bowl, pour the marinade over the top, and refrigerate 1 hour. Remove the chicken from the marinade and preheat oven to 375°F.

In a frying pan, heat olive oil over medium-high heat. When pan is hot, brown chicken on both sides, one half at a time. Remove and place in a shallow roasting pan, skin side up, and roast 30 to 35 minutes or until cooked through. You can check to see if the chicken is done by piercing the meat with a knife and seeing if the juice runs clear; if it is pink, then the chicken is not done yet.

Place the chicken on a carving board and cut it into serving pieces. Serve immediately.

PASTEL DE MAÍZ

Makes 6 servings

In old-fashioned Cuban kitchens, this velvety chicken-corn pie required a lot of arduous hand pureeing and mixing, but with the advent of food processors it is much easier to prepare. When you separate the egg yolks for this recipe, you can save the egg whites in a plastic container or Ziploc bag and freeze them for later use (up to 6 months).

Serve this delicious pie with rice and a tossed salad.

5 cups fresh corn kernels, cut
  from approximately 20 ears
½ cup (1 stick) butter
2 teaspoons sugar
1 teaspoon salt
2 pounds boneless, skinless chicken
  breasts
10 pitted prunes

1 tablespoon olive oil
1 cup finely chopped onions
3 cups peeled, seeded tomatoes
4 egg yolks
1 tablespoon softened butter for
  greasing baking dish
1 egg yolk, lightly beaten

Preheat the oven to 350°F. In the workbowl of a food processor, place 4 cups of the corn kernels, reserving 1 cup. Pulse 5 to 10 seconds, scrape the sides of the bowl, and pulse again until the corn is pureed.

In a medium-size saucepan, melt the butter over medium heat. Add the pureed corn and 1 teaspoon of the sugar. Stirring occasionally, cook for 20 to 30 minutes, until the mixture has thickened and will coat the back of a spoon. Transfer to a medium-size mixing bowl and set aside to cool.

Fill a deep pot a third full with water and add the salt. (Make sure there is enough water in the pot to cover the chicken breasts when added.) Bring the water to a boil over high heat. Add the chicken breasts, reduce the heat to medium, cover, and simmer 15 to 20 minutes, until cooked through. With a slotted spoon, remove the chicken to a plate and set aside to cool. Place the prunes in the hot chicken stock in the pot, let sit 15 minutes, then remove, pat dry, chop, and set aside.

In a large skillet, heat the oil over medium heat. Add the onions and sauté 1 minute. Sprinkle with the remaining teaspoon of sugar, cover, and simmer 4 to 5 minutes over low heat. Uncover and raise the heat to medium. Sauté gently to remove any excess liquid but not brown the onions. Drain and chop the tomatoes, then add to the onions. Again, remove any excess moisture by cooking over medium heat.

Chop the cooked chicken breasts into 1-inch cubes and stir into the tomato mixture. Add the prunes and the reserved 1 cup corn kernels, and set aside.

With an electric mixer, beat the 4 egg yolks until thick and light yellow in color. Add the pureed corn mixture and combine.

Grease a medium-sized baking or soufflé dish with the softened butter. Place half of the corn mixture in the bottom of the dish. Carefully place the chicken mixture over the pureed corn, spreading it smoothly and evenly. Cover with the remaining pureed corn mixture. Brush the top lightly with the lightly beaten egg yolk. Bake in the center of the oven for 1 hour, until the top is golden brown.

SOFRITO GRILLED CHICKEN
Pollo a la Parrilla con Sofrito

Makes 6–8 servings

This simple grilled chicken gains a unique flavor from being marinated in *sofrito*, the spicy Cuban sauce made from achiote oil. It can add an interesting new taste experience to a cook-out or picnic.

2 broiler chickens (about 2½
pounds each), cut into serv-
ing pieces
1 cup Sofrito Sauce (page 185)

Rinse the chicken and pat dry with paper towels. Rub each piece liberally with sofrito. Place in a glass dish, cover the dish with plastic wrap, and marinate in the refrigerator overnight.

Heat the grill. When the coals are medium-hot, remove chicken from the refrigerator and bowl, and place on the grill. Cook 15 minutes. Turn and cook 10 minutes more, until the chicken is tender and cooked through to the bone. Serve immediately.

SOFRITO SAUCE

Makes 1½ cups

This bright orange-red spicy sauce combines a base of achiote oil with some of the essential ingredients of Cuban cooking. It is used to flavor chicken dishes such as the grilled chicken on the opposite page, and also beef and pork dishes. Commercially prepared *sofrito* is also available. This homemade sofrito will keep up to two weeks covered in the refrigerator; the commercial variety has a much longer shelf life.

1 cup Achiote Oil (page 120)
2 green bell peppers, seeded, deribbed, and chopped
¼ cup mild green chilies, chopped
2 onions, chopped
6 garlic cloves, chopped
1 tablespoon chopped fresh oreg-
ano, or 1 teaspoon dried oregano
1 cup chopped fresh cilantro leaves, or 2 tablespoons dried cilantro
2 tomatoes, chopped
½ pound cured ham, chopped

Puree all the ingredients in a food processor. Place in a small saucepan and cook over medium heat for 15 minutes, stirring occasionally. Use in another recipe, or pour into glass jars, cover, and refrigerate until ready to use.

SEAFOOD

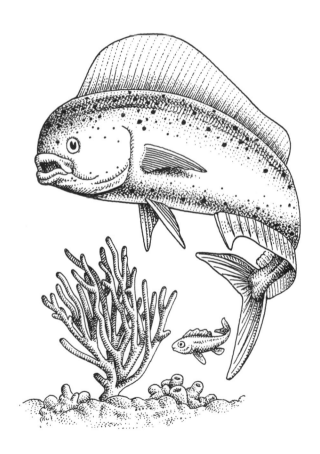

With thousands of miles of glorious coastline, Cuba is a fisherman's paradise. Marlin, bonefish, tuna, red snapper, and barracuda are just some of the species that lure deep-sea fishermen. Each year in late May, Cuba hosts the Ernest Hemingway Marlin Fishing Tournament. Fishermen from all over the world set out to catch white marlin from the Hemingway Marina, located west of Havana.

In Cuba, Ernest Hemingway is famous and highly respected for both his fishing talents and his writing talents. From 1939 to shortly before his death in 1961, he had an estate in a small town east of Havana. It is now a museum displaying his fishing trophies as well as his personal effects, manuscripts, and furniture. *The Old Man and the Sea*, Hemingway's story of a Cuban fisherman battling a giant marlin in the Gulf Stream, was set in the nearby fishing village of Cojimar. This classic novel immortalized Cuba's fishing heritage, which extends back to the Taíno Indians.

The Taíno Indians cooked their fish on wooden racks over outdoor fires. Columbus called these racks *barbacoa*, from which our term *barbecue* is derived. The Spaniards invented seafood dishes combining Spanish seasonings with tropical produce. Grouper, snapper, tuna, pompano, dolphin, lobster, shrimp, and conch are some of the species that were commonly cooked in Cuba. Since Florida shares the Gulf Stream waters with Cuba, these fish are also available in Miami, and Cuban-Americans now continue their culinary tradition of enjoying the fruits of the sea.

For tips on purchasing, handling, and cleaning fish and shellfish, see the Special Ingredients chapter.

PAN-FRIED GROUPER WITH ALMONDS
Mero a la Plancha con Almendras

Makes 4 servings

Grouper, which can grow as large as 500 pounds (although they are usually much smaller), thrive in warm waters around the world. Fresh grouper is regularly offered in Cuban restaurants in Florida, as it is in Cuba. This sweet fish has a thick skin that should always be removed before cooking. If you are in an area where fresh grouper is not available, a nice substitute would be snapper, or the popular orange roughy.

½ cup flour
1 teaspoon allspice
½ teaspoon salt
¼ teaspoon freshly ground black
   pepper
¼ teaspoon ground cumin

2 pounds boneless, skinless
   grouper fillet, cut into 4 pieces
1 tablespoon butter
¼ cup slivered almonds
¼ cup olive oil

In a medium-size mixing bowl, mix the flour, allspice, salt, pepper, and cumin. Rinse the fish fillets and pat dry. Run your fingers carefully over the fillets to feel for any bones and remove any you find with small or pin-nose pliers. Place the seasoned flour in a shallow plate. Dredge the fillets one at a time in seasoned flour, shaking off excess flour, then set aside.

In a large sauté pan, melt the butter over medium heat. Add the almonds and sauté until lightly browned, about 6 to 8 minutes, over medium heat, being careful not to burn. Transfer the almonds to a small saucepan and keep warm over low heat.

Heat the olive oil in a large sauté pan over medium-high heat. Add the fillets and fry until lightly browned, about 4 minutes on each side. Remove the fillets with a slotted spatula onto a warm serving platter. Spoon the almonds over the fillets, and serve.

SALT COD, ISLAND STYLE
Bacalao a la Criolla

Makes 4–6 servings

In the days before refrigeration, many types of fish were preserved for storage through the salting process. Cod can be purchased with or without bones, although the boneless variety is the most convenient. Dried salted haddock or pollock may be sutstituted for the cod.

Before using the fish, you must soak it in a covered bowl of cold water in the refrigerator for 6 hours or overnight. The water should be changed 2 to 3 times during the first few hours of the soaking process. Although soaking is preferable, if you don't have the time, you can place the fish in a pan of cold water, bring it to a boil, and simmer it for 1 hour, until the fish is tender and the salt is gone from it.

1 pound salted codfish (preferably boneless), soaked (see Headnote)
Butter for greasing baking dish
2 tablespoons butter
1 large onion, diced
2 garlic cloves, minced

1 tablespoon flour
½ cup white wine
1 cup water
1 tablespoon tomato paste
1 tablespoon minced fresh parsley
Salt and freshly ground black pepper to taste

Preheat the oven to 350°F. Carefully remove the fish skin and bones, if any. Lightly grease a glass baking dish with butter, place the fillets in it, and set aside.

In a medium-size saucepan, melt the 2 tablespoons butter over medium heat. Add the onion and garlic and sauté about 5 minutes, until soft but not brown. Mix in the flour and whisk until well blended. In a small bowl, whisk together the white wine, water, and tomato paste until there are no lumps. Add to the onion mixture. Add the parsley and mix well.

Pour the mixture over the fillets. (The tops of the fillets should be showing, with about a quarter of the fish not submerged in sauce.) Bake 30 to 40 minutes, until the tops are golden brown. Serve immediately.

BAKED SALT COD
Bacalao al Horno

Makes 4 servings

Salt cod was imported from Newfoundland into Spain and Portugal, where it was made into a number of dishes which then found their way to Cuba. This creamy cod, with its attractive garnish, looks appetizing with colorful side dishes such as yellow rice, peas, and red beans.

¼ cup olive oil
2 garlic cloves, minced
1 large onion, chopped
¼ cup white wine
1 tablespoon minced fresh chives
¼ cup butter
2 cups milk
2 pounds salted codfish (preferably boneless), soaked (page 192)

Olive oil for greasing baking dish
1 cup flour
1 teaspoon paprika
½ teaspoon freshly ground black pepper
Chopped chives and parsley sprigs for garnish

Preheat the oven to 350°F. In a medium-size saucepan, heat the olive oil over medium heat. Add the garlic and onion, and sauté until soft but not brown, about 3 to 4 minutes. Add the wine, cover, and reduce the heat to medium-low. Simmer 5 minutes. Stir in the chives and butter. When the butter is melted, stir in the milk, then remove from the heat and set aside.

Make sure the salt cod has no bones by running your hands over both sides of the fillet. Remove any bones with small or pin-nose pliers. Cut the fillet into serving-size pieces.

Grease a glass baking dish with olive oil. In a large bowl, mix together the flour, paprika, and pepper. Dredge the cod in the seasoned flour and place in the baking dish. Pour the milk and onion mixture over the fish and bake 30 to 35 minutes, just until the cod flakes. If the cod becomes dry during baking, add more milk. When the cod is cooked, place it on a large serving platter, garnish with chives and parsley, and serve.

BLACK-BEAN-STEAMED SNAPPER
Pargo al Vapor con Salsa de Frijoles Negros

Makes 4 servings

This lovely Cuban-Chinese snapper includes several ingredients which can be purchased in Oriental markets: fermented black beans, rice wine, and soy sauce (which is also sold in grocery stores). If you do not have a fish steamer, you can cook the fish on a rack placed in the bottom of a large pot over, but not in, boiling water. Possible substitutes for snapper are grouper, pompano, and halibut.

½ cup cooked black beans
  (page 96)
2 tablespoons fermented black
  beans
2 garlic cloves, minced
½-inch piece ginger root, minced
¼ cup soy sauce
1 teaspoon sugar

1 tablespoon peanut oil
2 pounds snapper fillet approximately ¾ inch thick in center, checked for bones (page 22)
¼ cup chopped scallions
2 tablespoons rice wine

In a medium-size mixing bowl, mix together the black beans, fermented black beans, garlic, and ginger by mashing the beans with the back of a fork. When the mixture is a paste, add the soy sauce, sugar, and oil, and mix well.

Rinse the fish and pat dry with paper towels. Put enough water in a fish steamer to almost touch the rack and bring water to a boil. Place the fish fillet on the steam tray and top evenly with the black bean mixture. Cover and steam 10 minutes, until the fish is done and flakes easily with a fork.

Toss the chopped scallions in the rice wine. Remove the fish fillet carefully with a spatula and place on a serving platter. Sprinkle with the scallions and wine and serve.

TUNA STEAK WITH SWEET RED PEPPER SAUCE
Rueda de Atún con Salsa Dulce de Ajíes Rojos

Makes 6 servings

Tuna is an oily fish, but it needs to be cooked with care to prevent it from drying out. The thick skin should be removed with a sharp knife and the tuna cooked until it is firm to the touch.

4 cups white wine
6 8-ounce tuna steaks, skin removed, checked for bones (page 22)
4 red bell peppers, seeded, deribbed, sliced in quarters lengthwise, and roasted (page 25)

6 shallots, peeled and left whole
½ cup heavy cream
1½ cups (3 sticks) butter, cut into 1-inch pieces

Preheat the oven to broil. In a roasting pan or broiling pan without a rack, place 2½ cups of the white wine. Place fish in wine and set aside. Puree the roasted peppers in a food processor. Place the puree in a small bowl and set aside.

In a small saucepan, combine the remaining 1½ cups wine and the shallots. Over medium heat, cook until almost all the wine has evaporated and only 2 tablespoons are left. Add the cream and reduce the heat to low. Cook until only about ¼ cup of the liquid is left. Remove the shallots with a fork and discard. Whisk in the butter, a piece at a time, until all the butter is blended in. Whisk in the pureed red peppers. Remove from the heat and keep warm in the top of a double boiler (avoid direct heat or the sauce will separate).

Broil the tuna steaks approximately 6 to 7 minutes, 2 to 3 inches from the heat source, until slightly firm to the touch. With a spatula, transfer the steaks to a warm serving plate. Top with about ¼ cup of the red pepper sauce and serve.

SNAPPER IN COCONUT SAUCE
Pargo en Salsa de Coco

Makes 6 servings

This creamy fish dish is similar to the Caribbean soup called *sopito*, except that the fish is not flaked and the liquid is thicker. Serve with white rice and black beans.

¼ *pound salt pork, cut into*
  small pieces
1 *onion, finely chopped*
2 *shallots, finely chopped*
1 *celery stalk, chopped*
1 *bay leaf*
2 *whole cloves*
¼ *teaspoon ground cumin*

¾ *cup fish stock (page 51)*
½ *cup freshly grated coconut*
  meat
½ *cup heavy cream*
1½ *pounds snapper fillets (3*
  large fillets cut in half, or
  6 small fillets), checked for
  bones (page 22)

In a medium-size saucepan, sauté the salt pork over medium heat until there is approximately 2 tablespoons of grease in the bottom of the pan. With a slotted spoon, remove the salt pork and discard. Add the onion, shallots, celery, bay leaf, cloves, and cumin to the grease and sauté until well cooked and lightly browned, approximately 8 minutes. Add the fish stock and stir together while scraping the bottom of the pan.

Strain through a sieve into a small bowl and discard the vegetables. Return the stock to the saucepan, cover, and turn off the heat. Puree the coconut with the cream in a food processor, pulsing 5 seconds at a time until smooth. Mix into the stock.

Lay the snapper fillets in a large sauté pan or skillet. Pour the coconut mixture over the fish, bring to a simmer over medium heat, then cook uncovered for 5 to 7 minutes.

With a spatula, remove the fillets to a warm serving platter or individual plates. Top with spoonfuls of coconut sauce, and serve.

LOBSTER AND RED PEPPERS IN A RICE MOLD
Langosta y Ajíes Rojos en Molde de Arroz

Makes 6–8 servings

Cuba has the largest lobster fishing industry in the Caribbean. The type of lobster caught in Cuba is called *langosta* in Spanish and spiny lobster in English. It has no claws, but the tail meat is known to be superlative. For this recipe, you can use either *langosta*, which is available in Florida and in some specialty markets, or Northern lobster.

3 cups fish stock (page 51)
2¼ cups white wine
2 cups long-grain white rice
¼ cup olive oil
1 red bell pepper, seeded, deribbed, and chopped, with a few julienned strips reserved for garnish
4 shallots, chopped
1 tablespoon minced garlic
1 tablespoon minced fresh basil (or 1 teaspoon dried)
½ teaspoon ground saffron
2 tablespoons minced fresh parsley
1 pound cooked lobster meat, cut into bite-size pieces

Preheat the oven to 400°F. In a large saucepan, bring the fish stock and wine to a boil over high heat. Reduce the heat to medium-low, add the rice, cover, and simmer 20 minutes.

Meanwhile, in a sauté pan, heat the olive oil over medium heat. Sauté the red pepper, shallots, garlic, basil, saffron, and parsley 2 to 3 minutes, until the red pepper is tender. Add the red pepper mixture and lobster meat to the rice. Stir until almost all the liquid is absorbed.

Have a 6-cup mold ready, preferably a ring-shaped mold with a nonstick surface. (If you do not have a nonstick surface mold, lightly grease the mold with olive oil.) Press the rice mixture firmly into the mold and bake 10 minutes.

Unmold onto a large serving platter by placing the platter on top of the mold and turning it upside down. Garnish with julienned strips of red pepper, and serve warm.

BROILED DOLPHIN WITH SWEET RED PEPPER AND PAPAYA CHUTNEY
Delfín a la Parrilla con Ajíes Rojos y Condimento de Papaya

Makes 6 servings

Many people confuse game fish dolphin with the mammals that are also called dolphins or porpoises; however, they are actually a different species. The type of dolphin that is commonly eaten—also called mahi mahi, dolphinfish, or dorado—is a beautifully colored green and yellow fish with small dark spots. Its firm white flesh is somewhat sweet and it is often served with sweet sauces, such as a citrus sauce or the French "Veronique" grape cream sauce. The sauce in this recipe combines red pepper and papaya to form a sweet chutney. If dolphin is not available, grouper may be substituted. This dish is nice to serve with warm buttered Cuban Bread (page 218).

½ cup diced red ripe papaya (be sure fruit is not over-ripe and too soft, and see page 24 before handling)
½ cup diced roasted red bell peppers (page 25)
½ teaspoon allspice
¼ cup malt or cider vinegar
1 small onion, finely diced
½ teaspoon salt
Dash of Tabasco sauce
1 cup water
6 8-ounce dolphin fillets (or larger fillets cut into 6 pieces), bones and skin removed (page 22)
White wine for broiler pan
Strips of roasted red pepper, julienned, for garnish (page 25)

In a medium-size saucepan over low heat, combine the papaya, roasted red pepper, allspice, vinegar, onion, salt, Tabasco sauce, and water. Cover and simmer for ½ hour. Remove from the heat and place the resulting chutney in a small glass serving dish. Let cool, then cover with plastic wrap and chill in refrigerator for at least 2 hours.

Preheat the oven to broil. Pour enough white wine in a

roasting pan or broiler pan without rack to fill it ⅛ inch deep. Add the dolphin fillets to the pan and broil 5 to 7 minutes, 2 to 3 inches from the heat source.

Transfer with a spatula to a warm serving platter. Place the dish of chutney on the platter. Garnish with roasted red pepper strips, and serve.

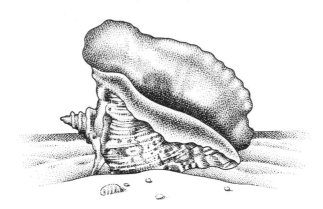

SHRIMP CREOLE
Camarones Creole

Makes 4 servings

Following Haiti's revolution in 1791, a large number of Haitian planters and slaves fled to Cuba. This shrimp dish is an example of the French Creole cooking which these immigrants introduced to Cuba. Serve it with white rice to soak up the sauce.

2 tablespoons butter
2 tablespoons olive oil
3 garlic cloves, minced
¼ cup chopped celery
¼ cup chopped onion
2 large tomatoes, peeled, seeded, and chopped
¼ teaspoon cayenne pepper (or more to taste)

1 tablespoon minced fresh parsley
½ teaspoon sugar
½ teaspoon salt
¼ teaspoon freshly ground black pepper, or more to taste
1½ pounds medium raw shrimp, peeled and deveined (page 27)
¼ cup white wine

In a large sauté pan, melt the butter with the oil over low heat. Add the garlic, celery, onion, tomato, cayenne pepper, parsley, sugar, salt, and black pepper. Cover, raise the heat to medium-low, and simmer 3 to 5 minutes, until the onion and celery are tender. Add the shrimp, cover, and cook 3 minutes. Add the wine and stir until the liquid comes back to a simmer. Remove from the heat and serve.

MARINATED CONCH SALAD
Ensalada de Cobo

Makes 6 servings

This conch is marinated in a tart lemon-lime juice mixture and it makes a sprightly, refreshing salad when served on a bed of crispy greens. Pound the conch vigorously with a wooden mallet before marinating, in order to make it more tender.

1 pound cleaned, pounded conch meat (page 21), cut into ½-inch pieces
½ cup diced onion
½ cup diced red bell pepper, seeded and deribbed
¼ cup diced celery
½ cup peeled, seeded, and diced cucumber

½ cup peeled, seeded, and chopped tomato
¼ cup lemon juice
¼ cup lime juice
½ cup olive oil
Salt and freshly ground black pepper to taste
Chopped fresh cilantro or parsley for garnish

In a large glass dish or ceramic bowl, toss the conch, onion, pepper, celery, cucumber, tomato, lemon juice, and lime juice. Cover the dish with plastic wrap and marinate in the refrigerator for 6 hours.

Toss the salad with the olive oil, salt, and pepper. Using a slotted spoon to drain off any excess marinade, serve on a bed of crisp greens, garnished with cilantro or parsley.

SEAFOOD STEW
Sopón a la Marinera

Makes 8 servings

In the Caribbean, the type of crabs often served are called *jueyes*, or land crabs, which must be purged before being eaten. Island chefs cleanse the crabs' innards by putting them on a three-day diet: the first day they're fed only coconut, the second day corn and water, and the third day only corn. In the United States, Cuban-Americans prefer to use the more wholesome sea crabs. For this briny stew, you can use either fresh or frozen crabmeat. Serve with a nice rice dish, such as yellow rice and peas, or plain white rice. You can also serve with a warm, freshly baked bread, such as Cuban Bread (page 218) or Spicy Red Pepper Muffins (page 233).

½ cup olive oil
2 garlic cloves, minced
1½ cups minced onions
¾ cup chopped green bell pepper, seeded and deribbed
¼ cup minced fresh parsley
⅛ teaspoon cayenne pepper
1½ cups peeled and seeded tomatoes
2 teaspoons tomato paste
3 cups fish stock (page 51)
1 cup white wine
1 teaspoon sugar

½ pound fillet of a white fish (flounder, sole, fluke, halibut, or cod), checked for bones (page 22)
¾ pound picked crabmeat (page 22)
½ pound medium raw shrimp, peeled and deveined (page 27)
¾ pound cooked lobster meat
¼ cup chopped fresh parsley or cilantro for garnish

In a large pot, heat the oil over medium-low heat. Add the garlic, onions, and green pepper and sauté until softened, about 5 minutes. Add the parsley, cayenne pepper, and tomatoes. Stir together over medium-low heat.

In a small bowl, whisk together the tomato paste and fish stock. Transfer to the pot containing the vegetables and add the wine and sugar. Bring to a simmer, cover, and cook 20 minutes.

Meanwhile, run your fingers up and down the fish fillet to check for bones and remove any you find with small or pin-nose pliers. Rub the crabmeat with your fingers to make sure there are no shell pieces or cartilage, and remove any you find.

After the stock has simmered 20 minutes, add the fish fillet to the pot and cook 3 minutes. Add the shrimp and cook 2 minutes. Add the lobster and crabmeat and cook 5 to 8 minutes, until hot through. Garnish with parsley or cilantro, and serve immediately.

BREADED SHRIMP WITH TOMATO-CAPER SALSA
Camarones Empanados con Salsa de Tomate y Alcaparras

Makes 21–25 shrimp
(4 entrée servings)

These breaded shrimp can be served on a warm platter with a bowl of salsa in the center and garnishes of parsley and lemon wedges. You can offer them as an appetizer or as a main course with Cuban Bread (page 218) and a bean salad.

BREADED SHRIMP:

1 cup flour
1 teaspoon salt
¼ teaspoon freshly ground black pepper
1 teaspoon paprika
⅛ teaspoon cayenne pepper

2 eggs
1 pound medium raw shrimp, peeled and deveined (page 27)
Vegetable oil for frying

SALSA:

¼ cup olive oil
4 garlic cloves, minced
1 onion, minced
¼ cup diced green bell pepper, seeded and deribbed
¼ cup mild diced canned green chilies
2 cups peeled and seeded tomatoes
1 tablespoon malt or cider vinegar

1 teaspoon sugar
2 tablespoons green capers
1 teaspoon cornstarch, mixed with 1½ tablespoons water
Salt and freshly ground black pepper to taste
Fresh cilantro sprigs or parsley, and lemon wedges, for garnish

In a medium-size bowl, mix the flour, salt, black pepper, paprika, and cayenne pepper. In another bowl, lightly beat the eggs. Place the bowls in your work area next to a rack for drying the shrimp.

Prepare the salsa so it can simmer while you are breading

the shrimp. In a saucepan, heat the oil over medium heat. Add the garlic, onion, and green pepper. Sauté approximately 5 minutes, until tender but not brown. Stir in the green chilies, tomatoes, vinegar, sugar, capers, and cornstarch and water mixture. Cover, reduce the heat to low, and simmer 15 to 20 minutes. Add salt and pepper to taste.

Meanwhile, one at a time, dip the shrimp in the beaten eggs, dredge in the flour until well-coated, then place on the rack.

Fill a deep fryer a third full with oil and heat to 375°F. and deep-fry the shrimp a few at a time for 3 minutes. (If you don't have a deep fryer, fill a large skillet a quarter full with oil, heat over medium heat and fry the shrimp for 2 minutes on each side.) Transfer to a plate lined with paper towels and let drain.

Place the shrimp on a warm serving platter with garnishments. Pour the salsa into a small bowl and place it in the center of the platter before serving. Serve hot.

SNAPPER WITH SAFFRON SAUCE
Pargo con Salsa de Azafrán

Makes 4 servings

Red snapper is abundant off the coast of Cuba and is often served for lunch or dinner. In this recipe the snapper is broiled in wine and topped by an ethereal saffron sauce. Serve with white rice.

¼ cup fish stock (page 51)
1 teaspoon saffron threads
1 cup white wine
5 shallots, finely chopped
4 garlic cloves, finely chopped

1½ cups heavy cream
2 pounds red snapper fillet,
  checked for bones (page 22)
White wine for broiling pan
2 tablespoons melted butter

Place the fish stock and saffron in a small saucepan. Bring to a boil over high heat, cover, turn off the heat, and steep 1 hour.

Meanwhile, pour the wine into a medium-size saucepan over high heat. Add the shallots and garlic and bring to a boil. Stir in the cream, reduce the heat to medium, and cook until the liquid has been reduced by half (approximately 10 minutes). Whisk in the fish stock and saffron after they have steeped 1 hour. Reduce the heat to low and keep stirring the sauce often while broiling the snapper.

Heat the oven to broil. Place the snapper fillets on the bottom of a broiling pan filled ⅛ inch deep with white wine. Run your fingers over the snapper fillets to feel for bones, and remove any you find with small or pin-nose pliers. Brush the fillets with the melted butter and broil 6 to 8 minutes, 2 to 3 inches from the heat source, until lightly brown on top and white through.

Transfer the fillets with a spatula to a warm serving plate. Top with some of the saffron sauce, and serve immediately. Place remaining sauce in serving dish or boat on table.

POMPANO WITH SHRIMP SAUCE
Pámpano con Salsa de Camarones

Makes 4 servings

This creamy shrimp sauce includes a splash of sherry which enhances the subtle sweetness of the pompano, a species that is found in the waters off Cuba and Florida. Yellow Rice (page 99), steamed green beans, and a light white wine are pleasant companions for the fish.

3 tablespoons butter
3 tablespoons flour
1 cup fish stock (page 51)
1¼ cups heavy cream
1 cup cooked shrimp, chopped
  (to cook shrimp, see page
  27)
2 tablespoons sherry

2 egg yolks
Salt and freshly ground black
  pepper to taste
2 pounds pompano fillet, checked
  for bones (page 22)
White wine for broiling pan
2 tablespoons melted butter
Pinch of paprika

In a medium-size saucepan, melt the 3 tablespoons butter over medium-low heat. Whisk in the flour and cook 2 to 3 minutes. Add the fish stock and whisk until smooth. Add the cream, shrimp, and sherry and whisk 6 to 8 minutes, until slightly thick.

In a small bowl, beat the egg yolks. While beating, slowly add ¼ cup of the shrimp sauce. Add another ¼ cup shrimp sauce to the yolks and mix well. Pour the sauce-yolk mixture into the saucepan with the remaining shrimp sauce. Remove from the heat, add salt and pepper to taste, and keep warm in the top of a double boiler, stirring often, while broiling the fish.

Heat the oven to broil. Run your fingers over the fish fillets to feel for bones and remove any you find with small or pin-nose pliers. Fill the broiling pan approximately ⅛ inch deep with wine. Place the fillets in pan and brush with the melted butter. Broil 6 to 8 minutes, until lightly brown on top and white through.

Transfer the fish to a warm serving plate. Top with the shrimp sauce and a pinch of paprika, and serve.

SPICY GRILLED TUNA
Atún Picante a la Parrilla

Makes 4 servings

This recipe offers a way to enliven fresh tuna with typically Cuban seasonings. You can serve this with a marinated black bean salad and warm Cuban Bread (page 218).

¼ cup olive oil
½ teaspoon salt
⅛ teaspoon cayenne pepper
¼ cup lemon juice
2 garlic cloves, minced
1 shallot, minced
½ teaspoon cumin powder

¼ cup chopped fresh cilantro sprigs, with a sprinkling reserved for garnish
2 pounds tuna fillet, checked for bones (page 22)
Vegetable oil for greasing grill
Lemon wedges for garnish

In a small mixing bowl, combine the olive oil, salt, cayenne pepper, lemon juice, garlic, shallot, cumin powder, and cilantro.

Place the tuna fillet in a medium-size glass or ceramic dish. Rub your fingers over the fish to feel for bones and remove any you find with small or pin-nose pliers. Pour the marinade over the tuna and marinate for 1 hour in the refrigerator, turning once.

Brush the grill with vegetable oil and heat to medium. Grill the fish 4 to 5 minutes on each side. Garnish with cilantro sprigs and lemon wedges, and serve.

SNAPPER GRILLED IN FOIL WITH CILANTRO, TOMATO, AND ONION
Pargo a la Parrilla con Tomate y Cebolla

Makes 4 servings

Since this snapper is cooked in foil, it makes an easy as well as succulent entrée for an informal outdoor supper, served with a side dish of Yellow Rice (page 99) and plenty of ice-cold beer. Instructions are given for both grilling and broiling the fish.

½ cup (1 stick) butter
2 pounds snapper fillet, checked
   for bones (page 22)
1 small onion, thinly sliced
1 small tomato, diced
2 garlic cloves, minced

1 tablespoon chopped fresh
   cilantro
1 lemon, cut in half, 1 half cut
   in wedges
3 tablespoons white wine

If you're using an electric grill, preheat to low. If using charcoal, light the coals (you will grill the fish over low-heat coals). If broiling, preheat the oven to broil.

Take enough aluminum foil to wrap the fish fillet and lightly rub the stick of butter over one side, using just enough to grease the foil lightly. Cut the remaining butter into ¼-inch-thick patties. Place the fillet in the center of the foil and dot with the butter pieces. Spread the onion, tomato, garlic, and cilantro on top of the fillet. Squeeze the juice from the lemon half over all, then sprinkle with the wine.

Roll the fish in the foil, sealing all edges, and grill 15 to 20 minutes, or broil, 2 to 3 inches from the heat source, for 10 to 12 minutes, or until the fillet has lost its translucence and is white through. Remove the fish from the foil, place on a warm serving platter with the lemon wedges, and serve.

POACHED POMPANO WITH ORANGE-RUM SAUCE
Pámpano Hervido con Salsa de Ron y Naranja

Makes 6 servings

This recipe utilizes the tangy flavor of fresh oranges, which are widely cultivated in both Cuba and Florida. Prepare the sauce first, since the fish will take only 10 to 12 minutes to cook. Serve with white rice, beans of choice and sweet fried plantains. You can also use this recipe with grouper or dolphin.

3 cups fish stock (page 51)
3 tablespoons butter
¼ cup flour
½ teaspoon ground ginger
¼ teaspoon dry mustard
¼ cup orange juice
2 tablespoons dark rum

2 tablespoons brown sugar
2 teaspoons grated orange peel
3 pounds pompano fillet, cut in
  6 pieces and checked for
  bones (page 22)
Orange slices for garnish

Place the fish stock in a fish poacher or a large pot. Cover and warm over medium heat. In a medium-size saucepan, melt the butter over medium heat. Add the flour and whisk together 2 to 3 minutes. Add the ginger and mustard and blend slowly. Whisk in the orange juice and rum. When hot, whisk in the brown sugar and orange peel. Turn off the heat and cover to keep warm.

Raise the heat under the fish stock to high. When the stock is boiling, place the fillet in the poacher or pot. Cover and cook over medium heat 10 to 12 minutes, until cooked through but not overcooked.

Remove the fillets with a spatula and transfer to a warm serving plate. Pat dry around the fish with a paper towel. Top with the orange-rum sauce and garnish with orange slices before serving.

SHRIMP WITH BLACK BEAN SAUCE
Camarones con Salsa de Frijoles Negros

Makes 4 servings

Cuban chefs use black beans to create thick, rich sauces, such as the one in this recipe, which could also be used with other meat and seafood dishes. The addition of soy sauce and ginger gives this sauce an intriguing Oriental edge. This type of recipe is often found on the menus of Cuban-Chinese restaurants in New York.

2 tablespoons butter
3 garlic cloves, minced
½ teaspoon ground ginger
2 large red bell peppers, seeded, deribbed, and chopped
1 tablespoon soy sauce
½ teaspoon ground black pepper
1½ cups white wine

½ cup chicken stock (page 52), mixed with 1 teaspoon cornstarch
1 cup cooked black beans (page 96)
2 pounds large raw shrimp, peeled and deveined (page 27)

In a medium-size saucepan, melt the butter over medium heat. Add the garlic, ginger, and bell pepper, and sauté for 5 minutes. Add the soy sauce, black pepper, wine, and chicken stock mixed with cornstarch. Stirring occasionally, cook the mixture until slightly thick, approximately 8 to 10 minutes. Stir in the black beans, reduce the heat to low, cover, and let sit, stirring occasionally, while making the shrimp.

In a large pot filled halfway with water, cook the shrimp over high heat until the water boils. Cook 5 minutes longer, then drain. Place the shrimp on a large warm serving platter, ladle the sauce over the top, and serve.

BREAD

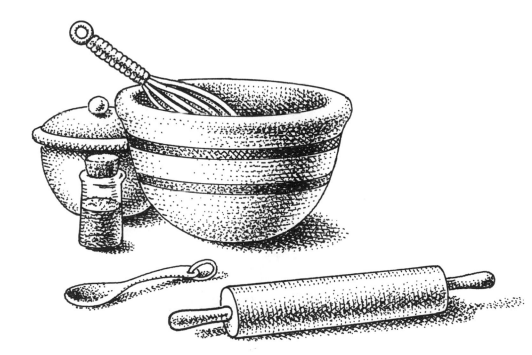

In Cuba, bread comes in many different shapes, textures, and flavors. But what is known as "Cuban bread" in the United States is a light, airy loaf with a plain taste that goes well with a wide variety of foods. In this chapter, you will learn to make Cuban bread, variations on this classic recipe, fruit-sweetened loaves, spicy breads, and cornbreads.

Baking bread is an experience that delights the senses: You feel the texture of dough, watch it rise, smell the aroma of the bread baking, and, best of all, taste the result. While it may be easier to purchase a loaf, there is something special about homemade bread. It fills the kitchen with a delicious fragrance; it shows your family and guests that you care; and it usually tastes far better than store-bought bread.

Unless otherwise specified, use all-purpose flour in these recipes. Use active dry yeast that has been stored in a cool, dry place for no longer than one year. Carefully follow the times allotted for the dough to rise, since variations can change the texture of the bread. Unsalted sweet butter is preferable from a flavor standpoint, but if you need to substitute margarine for health reasons, you may do so.

Homemade bread tastes best when it is eaten fresh, but it can be wrapped in aluminum foil or plastic and stored on the shelf for a few days, or in the refrigerator for up to a week. If you want to freeze a loaf, wrap it in plastic first, then in foil. Thaw the bread for 2 to 3 hours if you wish to serve it at room temperature. Bread will keep up to 6 months in the freezer. You can also reheat bread taken directly from the freezer by placing it in an oven preheated to 325° F. for 20 to 30 minutes.

CASSAVA BREAD
Pan de Casabe

Makes 2 loaves

The Taíno Indians used yuca, or cassava, to make a flat bread that was cooked on a griddle. Since this bread could be dried and saved up to two years, the Spaniards adopted it and used it on their long sea voyages. Today, cassava bread is still eaten, particularly with Ajiaco (page 83).

2½ cups flour
2½ teaspoons baking powder
2 eggs
½ cup olive oil
¼ cup milk

1 cup cooked, grated yuca (page 28)
1 tablespoon salt
Flour for dusting work surface

Preheat the oven to 450°F. Place a baking stone or cast iron griddle in the oven to preheat.

In a large mixing bowl, mix the flour and baking powder together and form a well in the center. Add the eggs, oil, milk, yuca, and salt. Stir with a wooden spoon until well blended, then place the dough on a lightly floured work surface and form into a ball.

Knead the dough 10 to 15 minutes, until it is smooth and elastic. (Or place the dough in the workbowl of a food processor and pulse 1 to 2 minutes, until smooth and elastic.)

Divide the dough in half and roll into flat circular loaves, about 1 inch thick. Remove the baking stone or griddle from the oven and place the loaves in the center. Place the baking stone or griddle back in the oven and bake 10 minutes, until the bread is very lightly golden brown. Cool the bread on a wire rack until warm enough to touch without burning your hands, and serve warm.

CUBAN BREAD
Pan Cubano

Makes 1 large loaf

This light, simple bread can be used to make sandwiches, to balance the flavor of spicy meat entrées, or to soak up fish sauces and rich soups, or it can be eaten alone spread with Mango Butter (page 235). Instructions are given to make the bread with a food processor or by hand.

1 envelope active dry yeast
2 teaspoons sugar
1½ cups lukewarm water
3 cups flour
1 tablespoon salt
2 tablespoons olive oil

Flour for dusting work surface
  (if making by hand)
Olive oil for greasing bowl and
  loaf pan
1 egg, beaten and mixed with
  1 teaspoon water, for glazing

TO MAKE IN FOOD PROCESSOR: In a small bowl, dissolve the yeast and sugar in ½ cup lukewarm water. Set aside for 3 to 5 minutes, until the mixture begins to foam. In a food processor with a steel blade, combine the flour and salt. Pulse to blend. When blended, turn the machine on and add the yeast mixture through the feed tube. Add the olive oil, then slowly add enough of the remaining lukewarm water so that the dough becomes smooth and forms a ball in the workbowl. (Be careful not to add too much water or the dough will become sticky.) Stop machine as soon as ingredients are blended so the dough does not get too tough.

Transfer the dough to a large, lightly oiled bowl. Cover with a damp cloth and let rise 30 minutes.

Punch down the dough and roll into a loaf shape. Place in a lightly oiled loaf pan and brush the top with the beaten egg and water mixture. Make 3 diagonal scores, ⅛ inch deep, across the top of the bread and bake 35 minutes. Remove the bread from the pan and place on a wire rack. Allow to cool before serving.

TO MAKE BY HAND: Dissolve the yeast and sugar in ½ cup

lukewarm water. Set aside 3 to 5 minutes, until the mixture begins to foam. In a large mixing bowl, combine the flour and salt. Make a well in the center and add the olive oil and yeast. Gradually add the remaining 1 cup of water as needed, so the dough holds its shape but does not become sticky.

Transfer the dough from the bowl to a lightly floured surface and knead for 4 to 5 minutes. Place the dough in a lightly oiled bowl, cover with a damp cloth, and let rise 30 minutes.

Preheat the oven to 400°F. Punch down the dough and roll into loaf shape. Place in a lightly oiled 8 × 5″ loaf pan and brush the top with the egg and water mixture. Make 3 diagonal scores, ⅛ inch deep, across the top of the bread. Place the bread in a cold oven and turn oven on to 400°F. Bake 45 to 50 minutes. Remove the bread from the pan and tap the bottom; if it sounds hollow, the bread is done. Place the bread on a wire rack. Allow to cool before serving.

TOMATO-PIMIENTO BREAD
Pan con Tomate y Pimientos Morrones

Makes 1 large loaf

The addition of pimientos and tomatoes makes this bread extra moist and turns it a vibrant color that brightens up the table. If you are making it by hand, follow the instructions for Cuban Bread (page 218) and add the tomatoes when you combine the flour and salt.

1 envelope active dry yeast
2 teaspoons sugar
1½ cups lukewarm water
3 cups flour
1 tablespoon salt
¼ cup diced pimientoes
¼ cup peeled, seeded, chopped, and well-drained tomatoes

2 tablespoons olive oil
Olive oil for greasing bowl and pan
1 egg, beaten and mixed with 1 teaspoon water, for glazing

In a small bowl, dissolve the yeast and sugar in ½ cup of the lukewarm water. Set aside for 3 to 5 minutes, until the mixture begins to foam.

In a food processor with a steel blade, combine the flour and salt. Pulse to blend. When blended, turn the machine on and add the yeast mixture through the feed tube. Add the pimientoes, tomatoes, olive oil, and enough of the remaining water so that the dough is smooth and forms a ball in the workbowl. (Be careful not to add too much water or the dough will become sticky.)

Transfer the dough to a large, lightly oiled bowl. Cover with a damp cloth and let rise 30 minutes. Preheat the oven to 400°F. Punch the dough down and roll it into a loaf shape. Place the dough in a lightly oiled 8 × 5″ loaf pan and brush the top with the egg-and-water mixture. Make 3 diagonal scores, ⅛ inch deep, across the top of the loaf. Let it rise again for 15 to 20 minutes, covered with a damp cloth in a warm spot. Then bake 35 minutes. Remove the bread from the pan and tap the bottom; if it sounds hollow, the bread is done. Place the bread on a wire rack to cool.

CHEESE BREAD
Pan de Queso

Makes 1 large loaf

This variation of Cuban Bread makes excellent sandwiches and also goes well with soup or stew. Instructions here are given for the food processor. To make the bread by hand, follow the instructions for Cuban Bread (page 218) and add the cheese when you combine the flour and salt.

1 envelope active dry yeast
2 teaspoons sugar
1½ cups lukewarm water
3 cups flour
1 tablespoon salt
¾ cup grated sharp white cheese
  (such as sharp white cheddar)

2 tablespoons olive oil
Olive oil for greasing bowl and
  loaf pan
1 egg, beaten and mixed with
  1 teaspoon water, for glazing

In a small bowl, dissolve the yeast and sugar in ½ cup lukewarm water. Set aside 3 to 5 minutes, until the mixture begins to foam. In a food processor with a steel blade, combine the flour and salt. Pulse to blend. Add the cheese and pulse again. When blended, turn the machine on and add the yeast mixture through the feed tube. Add olive oil and enough of the remaining water so that the dough is smooth and forms a ball in the workbowl. (Be careful not to add too much water or the dough will become sticky.) Transfer to a large, lightly oiled bowl, cover with a damp cloth, and let rise 30 minutes.

Preheat the oven to 400°F. Punch down the dough and roll into a loaf shape. Place in a lightly oiled 8 × 5″ loaf pan. Lightly brush the top with the egg and water mixture. Make 3 diagonal scores, ⅛ inch deep, across the top of the loaf. Let dough rise again for 15 to 20 minutes, covered with a damp towel in a warm spot. Then bake for 35 minutes. Remove the bread from the pan and tap the bottom; if it sounds hollow, the bread is done. Place the bread on a wire rack to cool before serving.

CASSAVA ROLLS
Panecillos de Casabe

Makes 24 rolls

The yuca gives these rolls a smoothly textured grain, a moist texture, and a subtle tang.

1 small yuca (4–5 ounces),
   peeled and cut in half (page
   28)
1 package active dry yeast
1 tablespoon plus ¼ teaspoon
   sugar
2 tablespoons warm water
1 cup milk

1½ teaspoons salt
4 tablespoons butter
3½ cups flour
1 egg, lightly beaten
Butter for greasing bowl and
   pans
1 tablespoon olive oil

Fill a small saucepan with enough water to cover the yuca and bring to a boil over medium-high heat. Add the yuca, cover, and reduce the heat to low. Cook 20 to 30 minutes, until the yuca is tender. Drain through a strainer, then transfer the yuca to a small mixing bowl. Mash with a fork or potato masher until the yuca is smooth, then set aside.

In another small mixing bowl, dissolve the yeast with ¼ teaspoon of the sugar in the warm water. Set aside until the yeast is foamy, approximately 5 minutes. Meanwhile, in a small saucepan over medium heat, heat the milk with the remaining 1 tablespoon sugar and the salt until near boiling. Remove from the heat, stir in the butter until melted, then stir in the mashed yuca.

In a large mixing bowl, combine 3 cups of the flour, the milk mixture, the yeast mixture, and the egg. Stir until well combined. Dust the surface of the dough well with the remaining flour and knead for approximately 8 minutes, until smooth and elastic. Transfer to a large, greased bowl. Cover with a warm, damp dish towel and let rise in a warm place for 1½ hours, until doubled in bulk.

Preheat the oven to 375°F. Lightly grease two 8″ round cake pans with butter. Punch down the dough and divide in half. Divide the halves in half and keep dividing the dough until there are 24 pieces. Shape each piece of dough into a round ball. Place the balls of dough in the cake pans, leaving about ¼ inch between each roll. Brush the tops of the rolls lightly with the olive oil. Let rise 30 minutes at room temperature before baking. Bake 25 to 30 minutes. Place the pan on a wire rack and let the rolls cool in the pan, then turn out and serve.

SWEET PLANTAIN BREAD
Pan de Plátano Dulce

Makes 2 loaves

Since Cubans usually eat just a light breakfast of coffee and bread, they customarily stop for another cup of coffee and a snack in mid-morning. This sweet plantain bread is a perfect coffee-break snack. It should be made with a very ripe, brown-black plantain. Spread with Mango Butter (page 235) if you like.

1 large ripe plantain
1 tablespoon butter
2¼ cups flour
1 teaspoon baking powder
1 teaspoon baking soda
½ teaspoon salt
½ cup butter, at room temperature

1 cup sugar
2 eggs
1 teaspoon vanilla
1 teaspoon lemon juice
Butter for greasing pans
Flour for dusting pans

Preheat the oven to 350°F. Peel and slice the plantain into 1-inch-thick diagonal slices (page 25). Melt the butter in a sauté pan over medium heat. When hot, add the plantain slices. Sauté 2 to 3 minutes on each side, just until soft. Transfer the plantain to a small mixing bowl and mash it well with a fork or potato masher, then set aside.

In a large mixing bowl, combine the flour, baking powder, baking soda, and salt. In a separate bowl, cream the ½ cup butter with the sugar. Beat in the eggs, then add the plantain, vanilla, and lemon juice. Add the plantain mixture to the dry ingredients and blend.

Grease two 8 × 5″ bread pans with butter and lightly dust them with flour. Pour the batter into the pans and bake approximately 1 hour, until a knife comes out clean when inserted into the bread. Remove from pan and allow to cool slightly on a wire rack before serving.

PAPAYA AND RAISIN BREAD
Pan de Papaya y Pasas

Makes 1 loaf

This bread uses tropical fruit, with raisins to add a Spanish touch. It is sweet enough to serve as a dessert or a snack. Be sure to use a papaya that is ripe, but not overripe and too soft, and check page 24 before handling it.

¾ cup chopped papaya (page 24)
½ cup raisins
¾ cup sugar
⅓ cup vegetable oil
2 eggs

⅔ cup milk
1 teaspoon baking soda
½ teaspoon salt
2¾ cups flour
Butter for greasing pan

Preheat the oven to 350°F. Place the papaya and raisins in a small mixing bowl. In a large mixing bowl, mix the sugar, oil, and eggs. Whisk in the milk and blend. Add the baking soda, salt, and flour. Gently mix in the fruit.

Pour the batter into a greased 8 × 5″ pan and bake 1 hour. The bread is done when the loaf shrinks slightly from the sides of the pan and is springy to the touch. Place the bread on a wire rack to cool slightly before serving.

ALMOND-RAISIN BREAD
Pan con Almendras y Pasas

Makes 1 loaf

This sweet, nutty loaf is moist and chewy. It is a treat with cream cheese or Mango Butter (page 235).

¼ cup (½ stick) butter, softened
¼ cup brown sugar
¼ cup granulated sugar
1 egg, beaten
2 cups flour
2 teaspoons baking soda
1 teaspoon salt

½ cup chopped almonds
1 cup raisins
½ teaspoon almond extract
½ teaspoon vanilla
Butter for greasing pan
Flour for dusting pan

Preheat the oven to 350°F. In a medium-size mixing bowl, cream together the butter, brown sugar, and granulated sugar. Beat in the egg. When blended, mix in the flour, baking soda, salt, almonds, raisins, almond extract, and vanilla.

Lightly grease an 8 × 5″ loaf pan and dust it with flour. Pour the batter into the pan and bake 50 minutes, or until the loaf shrinks slightly from the sides of the pan and is springy to the touch. Remove from the pan and cool slightly on a wire rack before serving.

ORANGE BREAD
Pan de Naranja

Makes 1 loaf

This slightly sweet bread is delightful at breakfast with a tall glass of fresh-squeezed orange juice.

¼ cup (½ stick) butter, softened
¼ cup granulated sugar
¼ cup brown sugar
2 eggs
½ cup orange juice
2 cups flour

2 teaspoons baking powder
½ teaspoon salt
1 tablespoon grated orange peel
½ teaspoon vanilla
Butter for greasing pan
Flour for dusting pan

Preheat the oven to 350°F. In a large mixing bowl, use an electric mixer to cream together the butter, granulated sugar, and brown sugar. Add the eggs and beat well. Add the orange juice and blend. Add the flour, baking powder, salt, orange peel, and vanilla.

Pour the batter into a lightly greased and floured 8 × 5″ loaf pan and bake 1 hour. When the loaf shrinks slightly from the sides of the pan and is springy to the touch, the bread is done. Place the loaf on a wire rack to cool slightly before serving.

SPICY CORNBREAD
WITH GREEN CHILIES
Pan Picante de Maíz con Ajíes Verdes

Makes 16 squares

This lively Cuban cornbread goes well with spicy soups, stews, and meat dishes. It can be prepared with hot or mild green chilies, depending the degree of hotness you prefer.

1 cup cornmeal
1 cup flour
2 tablespoons sugar
2 teaspoons baking powder
1 teaspoon salt
½ teaspoon freshly ground black pepper
1 egg, beaten

1 cup milk
¼ cup vegetable oil
¼ cup corn kernels (approximately 1 ear)
¼ cup canned mild or hot green chilies
¼ teaspoon cayenne pepper
Butter for greasing pan

Preheat the oven to 425°F. In a large mixing bowl, mix together the cornmeal, flour, sugar, baking powder, salt, and pepper. Make a well in the center of the mixture and add the egg, milk, oil, corn, chilies, and cayenne pepper.

Pour the batter into a 9-inch greased baking pan and bake 20 minutes, or until cornbread separates ever so slightly from the sides of the pan. Place the pan on a wire rack to cool slightly, then cut the bread into 16 squares and serve warm.

CHURROS

Makes 36 churros

Churros, deep-fried dough tossed with cinnamon and sugar, are a favorite snack in Cuba and Southern Florida. They are made in a special churros machine, which looks somewhat like a soft-serve ice cream machine. Since few people have such a machine at home, here is a way to make churros in a deep fryer. Five or six churros tossed with cinnamon and sugar make a tasty snack.

Vegetable oil for frying
2 eggs
1 cup sugar
1 cup milk
¼ cup melted butter

2 tablespoons baking powder
4 cups flour
Cinnamon and sugar for
 sprinkling

Fill a deep fryer with 2 to 3 inches of vegetable oil and heat to 375°F. In a large bowl, beat together the eggs, sugar, milk, butter, and baking powder. Add the flour slowly, 1 cup at a time, stirring well between each addition.

Fry dough, 1 tablespoonful at a time, in deep fryer for 7 minutes, turning so all sides are browned. Remove from the fryer with a frying basket or slotted spoon and let drain on paper towels. When all the churros are ready, place on a serving platter. Sprinkle with cinnamon and sugar, and serve warm.

SWEET CORNBREAD
Pan de Maíz Dulce

Makes 1 loaf

There are many different types of cornmeal, ranging from stoneground, which is very coarse, to finely ground. You can use any variety in this recipe, depending on the degree of grittiness you like in your cornbread. It will not have any other effect on the bread other than making it a bit more coarse, as long as you use cornmeal and not a corn flour. Serve the bread warm, with plenty of butter or honey.

1 cup flour
2 tablespoons sugar
1 cup cornmeal
½ teaspoon baking soda
½ teaspoon salt

1 egg, beaten
1 cup buttermilk
2 tablespoons melted butter
Butter for greasing pan

Preheat the oven to 450°F. In a large mixing bowl, combine the flour, sugar, cornmeal, baking soda, and salt. Make a well in the center of the mixture, and add the egg, buttermilk and melted butter. Mix together thoroughly, but do not overmix. Pour the batter into a lightly greased 9-inch baking pan.

Bake 18 to 20 minutes, until cornbread is light golden brown and separates ever so slightly from the sides of the pan. Place the pan on a wire rack to cool slightly. Serve the bread warm.

CORNMEAL BREAD
Pan de Maíz

Makes 1 loaf

This cornmeal bread is similar to New England's Anadama bread, except this Cuban version is made with brown sugar instead of molasses. It is a chewy, crusty loaf with a slightly coarse texture.

½ cup cornmeal	1 package active dry yeast
2 tablespoons brown sugar	4 cups flour
1 tablespoon salt	Flour for dusting work surface
2 tablespoons butter	Vegetable oil for greasing bowl
1¼ cups milk	Butter for greasing pan

In a large mixing bowl, combine the cornmeal, brown sugar, salt, and butter. In a small saucepan, scald the milk. Add ¾ cup of the hot milk to the mixture in the bowl and stir together.

Place the yeast in a small bowl. When the remaining milk is lukewarm, add to the yeast and let sit 8 minutes. Add the yeast mixture to the cornmeal mixture. Slowly add the flour, 1 cup at a time, until the dough is firm but not sticky. On a lightly floured surface, knead the dough 5 minutes, until smooth and elastic.

Place the dough in a lightly oiled bowl. Cover with a damp cloth and let rise 1 hour. Punch the dough down and roll into a loaf shape. Place it in a greased 9-inch loaf pan and let rise again until almost doubled. Meanwhile, preheat the oven to 375°F. Bake for 45 minutes. Remove from the pan and tap the bottom; if it sounds hollow, the bread is done. Place the loaf on a wire rack to cool slightly before serving.

COCONUT MUFFINS
Panecitos de Coco

Makes 1 dozen muffins

These muffins are a delicious Cuban coffee-break snack. When you are preparing them, do not overbeat the batter or the muffins can turn out rubbery. The batter should have some lumps remaining in it.

2 cups flour
3 teaspoons baking powder
1 teaspoon salt
2 tablespoons granulated sugar
1 tablespoon brown sugar
1 egg, beaten

1 cup milk
¼ cup melted butter
½ cup grated fresh coconut
  (page 20)
Butter for greasing muffin tins

Preheat the oven to 400°F. In a large bowl, mix together the flour, baking powder, salt, granulated sugar, and brown sugar. In a small bowl, whisk together the egg, milk, and butter. Make a well in the center of the dry ingredients and pour in the egg mixture. Stir together, using 12 to 15 long strokes.

Spoon the batter into greased muffin tins, filling the cups two-thirds full, and bake 20 minutes. To test for doneness, insert a cake tester into the center of one of the muffins. If it comes out clean, they are done. Remove the muffins from the tins and place on a wire rack to cool before serving.

SPICY RED PEPPER MUFFINS
Panecitos Picantes con Ajíes Rojos

Makes 12 muffins

These muffins have a speckled red dough that gives them an unusual appearance and flavor. They go well with black bean- or meat-based dishes and soups.

2 cups flour
3 teaspoons baking powder
3 teaspoons salt
½ teaspoon freshly ground black pepper
¼ teaspoon cayenne pepper
½ teaspoon paprika

2 tablespoons sugar
1 egg, beaten
1 cup milk
¼ cup melted butter
½ cup diced roasted red peppers (page 25)
Butter for greasing muffin tins

Preheat the oven to 400°F. In a large mixing bowl, mix together the flour, baking powder, salt, black pepper, cayenne pepper, paprika, and sugar. In a small bowl, whisk together the egg, milk, butter, and roasted peppers. Make a well in the center of the dry ingredients and pour in the egg mixture. Stir together, using as few strokes as possible. (Do not overbeat; the batter should have small lumps in it.)

Pour the batter into lightly greased muffin tins, filling each cup two-thirds full, and bake 20 minutes. To test for doneness, insert a cake tester into the center of the muffins. If it comes out clean, they are done. Remove the muffins from the tins and transfer to a wire rack to cool slightly before serving.

GARLIC-ONION DINNER MUFFINS
Panecitos con Ajo y Cebolla

Makes 12 muffins

These moist muffins are wonderful with rice and beans, Picadillo (page 121), or Ropa Vieja (page 119).

2 cups flour	1 cup milk
3 teaspoons baking powder	¼ cup melted butter
1 teaspoon salt	2 garlic cloves, minced
2 tablespoons sugar	1 medium onion, diced
1 egg, beaten	Butter for greasing muffin tins

Preheat the oven to 400°F. In a large mixing bowl, mix together the flour, baking powder, salt, and sugar. In a small bowl, mix together the egg, milk, butter, garlic, and onion. Make a well in the center of the dry ingredients and pour in the egg mixture. Mix together, using as few strokes as possible. (Do not overbeat; the batter should have some small lumps in it.)

Pour the batter into slightly greased muffin tins, filling them two-thirds full, and bake 20 minutes. To test for doneness, insert a cake tester into the center of one of the muffins. If it comes out clean, they are done. Remove the muffins from the tins and place on a wire rack to cool slightly before serving.

MANGO BUTTER
Mantequilla de Mango

Makes 1 cup butter

This luscious spread can be used on Cuban Bread (page 218) or any of the fruit loaves in this chapter. You can make papaya butter by substituting ¼ cup chopped papaya for the mango in this recipe. See pages 23 and 24 before handling the fruits. This butter will last one week in refrigerator.

½ *cup honey*
¼ *cup softened butter*
¼ *cup chopped mango (page*
  23)

In a medium-size mixing bowl, beat the honey, butter, and mango together with a wooden spoon or electric beater. Transfer to a small bowl and serve with bread.

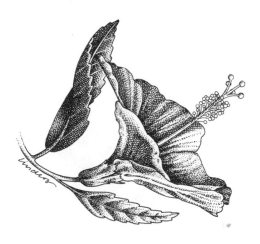

DESSERTS

After the Spanish conquistadors were largely unsuccessful in their attempt to find gold in Cuba, they began to cultivate cash crops, most notably tobacco and sugarcane. Between 1790 and 1830 the sugar trade boomed and nearly 700,000 slaves were imported to work on the plantations. The slaves hand-planted the sugarcane, wielded sharp machetes to cut the cane, and worked in wind-powered mills to produce massive amounts of raw sugar.

The exportation of sugar and its byproducts—molasses and rum—brought great wealth to the planters and traders. Besides reaping profits from the sugar, they enjoyed it in sumptuous desserts, such as flan (caramel custard), which originated in Spain. Flan recipes have been passed down from generation to generation and now Cuban-Americans continue the tradition of serving flan after festive dinners.

The sugar market fluctuated greatly over the centuries, but sugar is still Cuba's largest export. In Cuba, it is customary to indulge in sugary desserts after lunch and dinner. A common form of entertainment is to stroll out to buy ice cream at Coppelia, a major chain of ice cream shops on the island. In Miami, ice cream and other sweet desserts are just as popular.

In this chapter, you will learn how to make flans and puddings and other Cuban sweets. You will also learn how to make fresh tropical fruit ice creams at home. To do so, you need an ice cream maker. The hand-churning type makes wonderful ice cream, but it takes a great deal of time and effort. There are also expensive electric machines with built-in refrigeration systems. I recommend a midprice ice cream maker that does not have refrigeration but does have an electric churner.

DIPLOMATIC PUDDING
Pudín Diplomático

Makes 6—8 servings

This fruity, nutty pudding is a great way to turn Cuban Bread that has dried out into a special dessert. It can be served warm immediately after baking, or put into the refrigerator to chill.

1 loaf stale Cuban Bread, about 4 cups (page 218)	3 eggs
	2 tablespoons vanilla
4 cups milk	¼ cup chopped and well-drained fresh oranges
2 cups sugar	
1 tablespoon butter	¼ cup chopped almonds
2 tablespoons water	¼ cup chopped raisins

Crumble the bread into a large mixing bowl, pour the milk over it and let stand 1 hour. Meanwhile, have a 2-quart baking dish warming in a 200°F. oven.

In a small saucepan over medium-high heat, place ½ cup of the sugar, the butter, and the water. Stir until the mixture begins to bubble and turn a caramel-brown color. Remove the baking dish from the oven and pour the hot caramel into it. Roll the caramel around the dish to coat the sides. Set aside to cool.

Turn the oven up to 325°F. In another medium-size mixing bowl, beat together the eggs, the remaining 1½ cups sugar, and the vanilla. Stir the beaten eggs into the bread mixture. Add the oranges, almonds, and raisins. Pour the mixture into the prepared baking dish and bake on the middle rack of the oven for 1 hour. Cool slightly before serving, or cover with plastic wrap and chill in the refrigerator before serving.

TRADITIONAL FLAN
Flan Tradicional

Makes 6 servings

It is common for Cuban-Americans to proudly say, "My grand-mother makes the best flan you've ever tasted!" This creamy, smooth, light, sweet caramel pudding is a well-loved tradition, something special to look forward to at the end of a Cuban dinner.

1½ cups sugar
¼ cup water
2 ice cubes
2 cups milk

One 1-inch piece vanilla bean
One 1-inch piece lemon peel
3 eggs
¼ teaspoon salt

Preheat the oven to 350°F. Place 1 cup of the sugar in a small saucepan over medium heat with ¼ cup water. When sugar is melted, stop stirring and let simmer. Using a pastry brush dipped in water, wash the sides of the pan free of granular sugar. The sugar has caramelized when it turns slightly thicker and light brown in color. When this happens, add 2 ice cubes to stop the sugar from cooking, being careful not to get splattered with the sugar.

Have ready a heated 9-inch round glass baking dish or pie plate. (Heat by filling with boiling water, then draining and drying just before using.) Pour in the caramel and coat the dish by tipping it from side to side. Set aside.

In a small saucepan, scald the milk with the vanilla bean and lemon peel. Remove from the heat and let cool slightly. In a medium-size bowl, mix together the eggs, the remaining ½ cup sugar, and the salt. When the milk is slightly cool, remove and discard the vanilla bean and lemon peel. Add the milk to the egg mixture by whisking in slowly. Pour the mixture into the caramelized dish.

Place the baking dish in a pan filled with enough hot water to come halfway up the side of the flan dish. Bake 1 hour on the middle rack of the oven. (The flan is done when a knife inserted in the center comes out clean.) Remove from the oven and let cool slightly, until warm, before unmolding.

To ensure unmolding with caramel intact, dip the dish into a pan of hot water and let it sit 5 to 10 seconds. Then, place a serving platter on top of the dish, turn upside down, and lift up the dish. Serve the flan warm, or cover with plastic wrap and chill in the refrigerator before serving. Flan will last 3 to 4 days in the refrigerator.

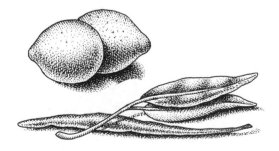

COCONUT-RUM FLAN
Flan de Coco y Ron

Makes 6 servings

Although flan originated in Spain, it is popular in Hispanic countries throughout the world, and each culture adds its own unique touches. Shredded coconut and rum lend a Cuban flavor to this variation.

2 cups milk
2 whole eggs plus two egg whites
½ cup sugar
¼ teaspoon salt

2 tablespoons dark rum
½ cup grated or shredded fresh
*   coconut (page 20)*

Preheat the oven to 350°F. In a small saucepan, scald the milk. Remove from the heat and let cool slightly. In a medium-size bowl, beat the eggs, sugar, salt, and rum together. In a slow, steady stream, pour the milk into the egg mixture, whisking constantly. Stir in the coconut.

Pour the mixture into a 9-inch round glass baking dish or pie plate, or 6 individual custard cups. Place the dish or cups in a pan of hot water, enough to come halfway up the sides of the flan dish. Bake on the middle rack of the oven for 1 hour, until a knife comes out clean when inserted in the center. (The custard cups will take 20 to 30 minutes.)

Let cool just until warm before unmolding. To unmold, place a serving platter over the dish or cups and turn upside down, lifting up on the dish or cups. Serve warm, or cover with plastic wrap and chill in the refrigerator before serving.

COUNTRY-BAKED ALMOND FLAN
Flan al Horno con Almendras

Makes 6 servings

This flan is heartier than most, with the almonds adding substance and texture. The process of baking the flan with flour gives it a firm, country-style consistency.

1¼ cups milk
⅔ cup sugar
3 eggs
1 teaspoon vanilla
⅔ cup flour
½ cup slivered almonds (no skins)

½ teaspoon almond extract
2 tablespoons brown sugar, plus more for sprinkling
Butter for greasing dish

Preheat the oven to 350°F. In the workbowl of a food processor, place the milk, sugar, eggs, vanilla, flour, almonds, almond extract, and brown sugar. Pulse 5 to 10 seconds at time, pausing to scrape the sides of the bowl, until the mixture is blended but not overprocessed.

Pour the batter into a lightly greased 9-inch round glass baking dish or pie plate. Bake for 30 minutes, until slightly puffy and brown. (A knife will come out clean when inserted in the center.) Sprinkle with brown sugar and let cool slightly before serving.

PLANTAIN CUSTARD
Flan de Plátano Maduro

Makes 6 servings

This custard is spiced with nutmeg, which grows on tall trees in the Caribbean (principally in Grenada). As the nuts ripen on these trees, their spongy outer layers open and the nutmegs conveniently drop to the ground. The nutmegs are covered with a red webbing called mace, which is stripped off and cured into a different spice.

1 tablespoon butter
2 very ripe, brown plantains,
    peeled and cut into 1-inch-thick
    diagonal slices (page 25)
1 teaspoon lemon juice
¼ cup sugar

½ teaspoon grated nutmeg
½ teaspoon ground cinnamon
2 whole eggs and 2 egg whites
1 teaspoon vanilla
2 cups milk

Preheat the oven to 350°F. Melt the butter in a medium-size sauté pan over medium heat. Add the plantains and sauté 2 to 3 minutes on each side, just until soft. Remove from the heat, transfer the plantains to a medium-size mixing bowl, and mash with a fork or potato masher.

Transfer to a large mixing bowl and mix with the lemon juice, sugar, nutmeg, cinnamon, eggs, and vanilla, blending well. Scald milk in a small saucepan and temper egg mixture by slowly adding hot milk in a slow steady stream while whisking to raise the temperature of the eggs without curdling. Then mix well. Transfer the flan to 6 individual custard cups or a 9-inch round glass baking dish or pie plate. Place in a pan of hot water to come halfway up the sides of the custard and bake on the middle rack of the oven for 1 hour (20 to 30 minutes for the custard cups), or until a knife inserted in the center comes out clean.

Remove the dish or cups from the pan of water and allow to cool slightly, then invert one at a time onto a small plate. Slide the flan onto a serving platter, let cool, and cover with plastic wrap. Chill in the refrigerator before serving.

FROZEN RUM MOUSSE
Mousse Congelado de Ron

Makes 6 servings

This is a light, sophisticated dessert with a creamy texture and a nuance of rum. You may serve it plain or top it with dark chocolate shavings and a sprig of fresh mint or slices of fresh fruit.

2 cups milk	1 envelope unflavored gelatin
4 egg yolks	¼ cup dark rum
1 cup sugar	½ pint heavy cream

Heat the milk in a medium-size saucepan over medium-low heat. In a small bowl, whisk together the egg yolks, sugar, and gelatin. Temper the egg mixture by adding some of the hot milk in a slow steady stream while whisking to raise the temperature of the eggs without curdling. Then return to the saucepan and mix well. Continue to whisk the mixture over low heat until it thickens slightly and coats the back of a spoon. Remove from the heat and transfer the mixture to a bowl. Stir in the rum and let cool. Cover with plastic wrap.

Whip the cream and fold it into the cooled mixture. Pour the mousse into a mold or glass bowl and chill in the refrigerator 2 to 4 hours, until firm.

To unmold, dip the mold into hot water for 20 to 30 seconds, letting the water come as high as the mousse. Place a serving platter over the mold, turn it upside down, and lift up on the mold or bowl. Serve very cold.

BAKED RUM-RAISIN PUDDING
Pudín al Horno con Pasas y Ron

Makes 6 servings

Raisins and rum add body to this cornmeal pudding, which has a pleasingly thick, substantial consistency.

3½ cups milk
2 teaspoons butter
½ teaspoon salt
⅓ cup sugar
½ cup cornmeal

4 eggs
1 tablespoon dark rum
¼ cup raisins
Butter for greasing dish

Preheat the oven to 375°F. In a medium-size saucepan over medium-low heat, warm the milk, whisking constantly. Add the butter, salt, sugar, and cornmeal. Continue to whisk constantly until the mixture is smooth and thick and can coat the back of a spoon, then remove from the heat.

In a small bowl, whisk together the eggs and rum. Slowly whisk in ½ cup of the milk mixture. In a slow, steady stream, pour the egg mixture into the saucepan with the milk mixture, whisking constantly. Add the raisins and mix until well combined.

Pour into a greased 8″ round pudding dish and bake 35 to 40 minutes, until set. Allow to cool slightly, slice, and serve warm.

CLASSIC RICE PUDDING
Pudín de Arroz

Makes 6 servings

This rice pudding recipe is versatile as well as delicious. You can serve it warm right out of the oven, or chill it and serve it topped with fresh tropical fruit such as papaya or mango, or guava.

2 cups cooked long-grain white rice (page 95)
1½ cups milk
¼ teaspoon salt
⅓ cup sugar
1 tablespoon butter, softened

1 teaspoon vanilla
4 eggs, lightly beaten
¼ cup raisins (optional)
¼ cup brown sugar
Butter for greasing baking dish

Preheat the oven to 325°F. In a medium-size mixing bowl, combine the rice, milk, and salt. In another mixing bowl, cream the sugar and butter, then add the vanilla and eggs. Stir in the raisins, if desired. Add the rice and milk to the egg and sugar mixture and mix well.

Pour the mixture into a greased glass baking dish and bake 50 minutes, until set. Remove from the oven and sprinkle with the brown sugar. Serve warm, or cover with plastic wrap and chill in the refrigerator before serving.

OLD-FASHIONED CORNMEAL PUDDING
Pudín de Harina de Maíz a la Antigua

Makes 6 servings

This cornmeal pudding is not overly sweet and it's relatively easy to prepare as long as you don't mind stirring. Serve it when you want a simple dessert to follow a heavy, spicy lunch or dinner.

4 cups water
1 cup milk
2 tablespoons brown sugar

1 teaspoon vanilla
2 cups cornmeal
2 tablespoons butter

While stirring, bring the water, milk, brown sugar, and vanilla to a boil in a medium-size pot over medium-high heat. Slowly pour in the cornmeal, stirring constantly. Turn the heat down to medium and stir 10 to 15 minutes, until the mixture is smooth and thick.

Add the butter and stir until the butter melts. Pour the pudding into a warm ceramic bowl and serve immediately, or keep it in the pot, covered, until ready to eat.

BACON FROM HEAVEN
Tocino del Cielo

Makes 8 servings

This almond cake came to Cuba from Portugal, where it is believed to have originated as far back as the fifteenth century. The origin of the intriguing name is obscure. Some food historians believe the recipe was first made in a convent and actually contained bacon. Others believe the name expresses the idea that in heaven even a simple food like bacon is transformed into something as sweet and delicious as this cake.

1 tablespoon butter, softened
1¾ cups plus 2 tablespoons sugar
½ cup water
1¾ cups blanched almonds, finely
  ground

8 egg yolks and 3 whole eggs,
  beaten together

Preheat the oven to 350°F. Grease an 8-inch cake pan with the softened butter. Sprinkle the pan with 2 tablespoons of the sugar and tip from side to side to coat. Turn the pan upside down to discard any excess sugar. Set the pan aside.

In a medium-size saucepan over medium heat, mix the remaining 1¾ cups sugar and the water and stir until the sugar is dissolved. Add the ground almonds and continue to stir until the mixture has thickened and is translucent. Remove the saucepan from the heat and slowly whisk in the beaten eggs, pouring in a steady stream while whisking continuously, until all the egg has been added.

Return the saucepan to low heat and stir constantly until the mixture has thickened, approximately 10 minutes. Place the prepared cake pan in a large roasting pan filled halfway with warm water. Pour the cake mixture into the cake pan.

Bake on the middle rack of the oven for 30 to 40 minutes, until the cake is firm to touch. Carefully remove the pan from the oven and set onto a wire rack. Let stand and serve at room temperature, or let stand, cover, and chill before serving.

FRIED YUCA DOUGH
WITH ALMOND SYRUP
Buñuelos de Yuca con Sirope de Almendras

Makes 16 servings

Here is another way the versatile yuca is used in Cuban cooking: to make a moist fried dough dessert. You may also save the dough that has been cooked, place in a plastic bag, and refrigerate for breakfast the next morning.

1 cup mashed yuca (page 28)	1 teaspoon baking soda
2 eggs	½ teaspoon salt
⅔ cup sugar	1 cup sugar
1 cup milk	½ cup water
2 tablespoons melted butter	½ teaspoon vanilla
4 cups flour	¼ cup slivered almonds
2 teaspoons baking powder	Vegetable oil for deep frying

In a medium-size mixing bowl, mix the mashed yuca and eggs. Mix in the ⅔ cup sugar, milk, and melted butter. In a large mixing bowl, mix together the flour, baking powder, baking soda, and salt. Add the yuca mixture to the dry ingredients and stir until well blended. Cover the bowl with plastic wrap and chill in the refrigerator.

Meanwhile, in a small saucepan over medium-low heat, combine the 1 cup sugar, water, and vanilla. Stir the mixture until it forms a thick syrup, approximately 10 minutes. Add the almonds, mix together, cover, and set aside.

Preheat the oil in a deep fryer to 375°F. Place the dough, 1 heaping tablespoonful at a time, into the deep fryer. Fry 3 to 4 pieces of dough at a time until lightly golden brown, approximately 6 to 8 minutes. Remove the fried dough and drain on paper towel.

When ready to serve, spoon some of the almond syrup onto the bottom of small dessert plates. Place 1 piece of fried dough on top of the syrup on each plate, and serve hot.

ALMOND COOKIES
Galleticas de Almendras

Makes approximately 24 cookies

These cute little ball-shaped cookies are buttery and delicate. You can serve them fresh out of the oven with Cuban coffee or save them in a cookie jar — although if you have children, they won't last long!

3/4 cup butter, softened
1 cup sugar
1 egg
1 tablespoon vanilla
1/2 teaspoon almond extract

2 cups flour
1/2 teaspoon salt
1/2 cup chopped almonds
Powdered sugar for rolling
  cookies

Preheat the oven to 350°F. In a large bowl, cream together the butter and sugar. Beat in the egg, vanilla, and almond extract. Add the flour, salt, and almonds, and combine.

Roll the dough into balls approximately 1 inch in diameter. Place on an ungreased cookie sheet and bake 15 to 20 minutes, until lightly browned. Remove from the oven and transfer to a wire rack to cool slightly. When cool enough to handle, roll the cookies in powdered sugar, then serve warm or place on another rack to dry.

FRESH COCONUT AND BANANA CREAM PIE
Pastel de Plátano y Coco

Makes 1 pie

Cuban-Americans, in their generous and hospitable fashion, often give each other gifts of food. This heavenly pie makes a splendid gift, or it can crown a special dinner you serve at home.

CRUST:
1½ cups flour
½ teaspoon salt
½ cup butter

3–4 tablespoons water
Flour for dusting work surface

FILLING:
3 cups milk
1 tablespoon vanilla, mixed with
   2 tablespoons water
¾ cup sugar
¼ cup cornstarch
¼ teaspoon salt

4 egg yolks
2 medium ripe bananas
½ lemon
⅓ cup grated fresh coconut (page
   20)

TOPPING:
½ pint heavy cream
1 teaspoon vanilla

¼ cup sugar
¼ cup coconut flakes

CRUST: Preheat the oven to 425°F. In a bowl, combine the flour and salt. Using a pastry blender or the back of a fork, cut in the butter until the mixture resembles a coarse meal. Sprinkle in the water, 1 tablespoon at a time, and toss lightly until the dough holds its shape when formed into a ball.

Roll the dough out approximately ¼ inch thick on a lightly floured surface in a circular shape. Place the dough in a 9-inch pie plate. (If the dough does not transfer easily, fold it in half, then in half again; pick it up and place it in the pie plate, then unfold.) Prick the dough in 4 spots with a fork to allow the steam to escape and the crust to bake. Bake 6 to 7 minutes, until lightly browned but not fully cooked. Remove from the oven and set aside.

FILLING: In a medium-size saucepan over medium-low heat, stir or whisk together the milk, vanilla, sugar, cornstarch, and salt. Whisk continually until the mixture is hot and almost at a boil. Beat the egg yolks in a small bowl, and slowly pour in ½ cup of the hot milk, whisking constantly. Pour the egg mixture back into the saucepan in a slow, steady stream, whisking constantly. Stir over medium heat until the mixture is thickened and hot, then remove from the heat.

Peel 2 bananas and slice thinly. Squeeze the juice from the lemon half into a medium-size bowl and toss the bananas in it. Set aside. Stir the coconut into the filling mixture.

Place the bananas on the cooled pie crust, pour the filling over them, and chill the pie, covered with plastic wrap, in the refrigerator approximately 2 to 3 hours.

TOPPING: While the pie is cooling, prepare the topping. In a bowl with an electric mixer, whip the cream with the vanilla and sugar until soft, glossy peaks form. Heat the oven to broil. On a cookie sheet, toast the coconut flakes for 4 to 5 minutes on a sheet pan approximately 2 to 3 inches from the heat source. (A toaster oven will work just as well.)

Spread the whipped cream over the top of the pie and sprinkle with the toasted coconut flakes. Slice and serve cold.

SPONGE CAKES WITH RUM
Torta Esponjosa de Ron

Makes 6 small cakes

These light little cakes have a soft, spongy texture. Serve them with iced coffee for a snack, or topped with vanilla ice cream for dessert.

3 eggs, separated	*Butter for greasing muffin tin*
⅓ cup sugar	*Flour for dusting muffin tin*
½ teaspoon salt	*½ cup dark rum*
⅓ cup flour	*½ cup honey*

Preheat the oven to 350°F. In a bowl with an electric mixer, beat the egg whites until stiff. In a separate bowl, beat together the egg yolks, sugar, salt, and flour. Fold the egg whites into the batter. Pour the mixture into 6 greased, floured muffin cups and bake 20 minutes, until light brown.

While the muffins are baking, warm the rum and honey in a small saucepan over medium-low heat. When the cakes are done, remove from the muffin tin, dip top and bottom of each cake in the rum mixture, and serve immediately. If not serving immediately, remove cakes from tin when cooled slightly and wrap with plastic wrap until ready to use. They should not be made more than 12 hours in advance or they become slightly dry.

VANILLA BEAN ICE CREAM
Mantecado de Vainilla

Makes 6 servings or 1 quart

If you think vanilla ice cream is dull, you won't after you sample the superior flavor of the fresh, homemade variety. It tastes great plain, or topped with warmed chocolate syrup or fresh fruit. For an elegant treat, top it with Flaming Mango Sauce (page 258).

1 cup milk
¾ cup sugar

1 vanilla bean
3 cups heavy cream, chilled

In a medium-size saucepan over medium-low heat, warm the milk with the sugar and vanilla bean. When hot but not boiling, remove from the heat and allow to cool.

Remove the vanilla bean and slice it in half lengthwise. Scrape out the seeds in the center of the bean and place in a bowl with the cooled milk and the cream. Mix well.

Pour the mixture into an ice cream maker (page 239) and follow the manufacturer's instructions.

FLAMING MANGO SAUCE OVER HOMEMADE VANILLA ICE CREAM
Mantecado de Vainilla Hecho en Casa con Salsa de Mango

Makes 6 servings

This flamboyant dessert will dazzle your dinner guests, yet it is actually quite easy to make. It is best with homemade ice cream, although a premium store-bought variety may be substituted.

1 cup diced mango (page 23)
½ cup sugar
½ cup water
¼ teaspoon cinnamon

1 quart Vanilla Bean Ice Cream
  (page 257)
½ cup dark rum

In a small sauté pan over medium-high heat, bring the mango, sugar, water, and cinnamon almost to a boil. Lower the heat to medium and stir continuously for 3 to 4 minutes, until the sauce thickens slightly. Warm the rum in a small pan.

Transfer the sauce to a heatproof bowl and bring it and the pan of warmed rum to the dining table. Place the ice cream in individual serving bowls in front of the guests. Dim the lights, then ignite the rum with a match and pour it into the mango sauce. When the flames die, spoon the sauce over the ice cream.

FROZEN BANANA CUSTARD
Pudín Congelado de Plátano

Makes 6 servings

The eggs make this luscious frozen custard even creamier and richer than ice cream. You can top it with fresh banana slices and whipped cream to make a deluxe banana sundae, if you wish.

2 cups milk
4 eggs
½ cup sugar

1 teaspoon vanilla
3 large, ripe bananas, peeled

In a small saucepan, bring milk to a boil over medium-high heat, remove from heat, and let cool slightly.

In a medium-size saucepan over medium-low heat, whisk together the eggs, sugar, scalded milk, and vanilla. Whisk constantly until the mixture thickens and coats the back of a spoon, then remove from the heat.

In a food processor, puree the bananas. Add the warm milk and egg mixture. Pulse 2 to 3 times for 5 seconds, then stop and scrape the sides of the bowl.

Allow the custard to cool to room temperature. Pour the custard into an ice cream maker (see page 239) and follow the manufacturer's directions.

COCONUT ICE CREAM
Helado de Coco

Makes 6 servings

Coconut ice cream is a favorite Cuban flavor. It has a cool, refreshing taste that's perfect on a hot summer night.

4 cups heavy cream
¾ cup sugar
1 teaspoon vanilla

½ cup toasted coconut flakes
(page 20)

In a medium-size saucepan over medium-low heat, warm 1 cup of the cream with the sugar and vanilla. When hot but not boiling, remove from the heat and let cool slightly.

Add the remaining 3 cups cream and the coconut to the mixture, and stir together. Pour into an ice cream maker (see page 239) and follow the manufacturer's directions.

MANGO ICE CREAM
Helado de Mango

Makes 6 servings

One of the fun things about having your own ice cream maker is that you can make flavors that are not always available commercially. This mango ice cream is an exotic fruity treat.

2 cups milk	½ teaspoon vanilla
4 eggs	1 cup chopped mango (page 23)
¾ cup sugar	

In a small saucepan, bring milk to a boil over medium-high heat, remove from heat, and let cool slightly.

In a medium-size saucepan, whisk together the eggs, sugar, scalded milk, and vanilla. Place over medium-low heat and whisk constantly until hot but not boiling. Remove the mixture from the heat and allow to cool slightly.

In a food processor, puree the mango. Add the cream mixture. Pulse 2 or 3 times for 5 seconds, then stop and scrape the sides of the bowl until blended.

Pour the mixture into an ice cream maker (see page 239) and follow the manufacturer's directions.

PINEAPPLE ICE CREAM
Helado de Piña

Makes 6 servings

This homemade pineapple ice cream has a clean, refreshing taste. Serve it with wedges of fresh pineapple on top, if you wish.

2 cups milk
4 eggs
¾ cup sugar

½ teaspoon vanilla
½ cup chopped fresh pineapple, patted dry of excess liquid

In a small saucepan, bring milk to a boil over medium-high heat, remove from heat, and let cool slightly.

In a medium-size saucepan, whisk together the eggs, sugar, scalded milk, and vanilla. Place over medium-low heat and whisk constantly until the mixture is hot but not boiling, and is thick enough to coat the back of a spoon. Stir in the pineapple, then set aside and allow to cool.

When cool, place in an ice cream maker (see page 239) and follow the manufacturer's directions.

GUAVA ICE CREAM
Helado de Guayaba

Makes 6 servings

Guava is a fruit native to Cuba and was eaten raw by the Taíno Indians. This recipe uses sweetened guava puree, which is available in many health food stores and Hispanic markets.

2 cups milk
4 eggs
½ cup sugar

½ teaspoon vanilla
1 cup sweetened guava puree
(see headnote)

In a small saucepan, bring milk to a boil over medium-high heat, remove from heat, and let cool slightly.

In a medium-size saucepan whisk together the eggs, sugar, scalded milk, and vanilla. Place over medium-low heat and stir or whisk constantly until the mixture is hot but not boiling, and thick enough to coat the back of a spoon.

Stir in the guava puree, remove from the heat, and allow to cool. Pour into an ice cream maker (see page 239) and follow the manufacturer's directions.

BEVERAGES

Coffee is extremely popular in Cuba, where it has been cultivated for hundreds of years. Many Cubans drink coffee at breakfast, in the mid-morning, after lunch, in the late afternoon, and again after dinner. The best Cuban coffee comes from the Pinar del Rio province, a dramatically beautiful area with vertical limestone cliffs and nutrient-rich soil.

Because of the trade embargo, Cuban coffee is not available in the United States. But many Cuban-Americans still drink plenty of strong coffee, favoring Jamaican espresso grinds. This chapter will tell you how to prepare coffee Cuban-style.

In both Cuba and Miami, an abundance of fresh fruit is available and cooling fruit juice milk shakes, called batidos, are very popular. You will learn how to make these ambrosial fruit drinks in your blender at home.

Surprisingly, beer is actually the most popular alcoholic beverage in Cuba, not rum, and fresh, malty Cuban brews are often consumed at lunch and dinner. However, in this chapter we will focus on cocktails made with rum, the drink most commonly associated with Cuba.

Rum is made from sugarcane and has been produced in Cuba since the seventeenth century. Light rum was developed in Cuba's famous Bacardi distillery in the late nineteenth century. When Prohibition took hold in the United States, bartenders as well as thirsty tourists began to flock to Cuba, and Havana became known as the cocktail capital of the world. A number of exotic concoctions were invented by Havana's illustrious bartenders, cocktails that are now favorites of rum lovers everywhere.

CUBAN COFFEE
Café Cubano

Makes 4 servings

Cuban coffee is usually double the strength of American coffee and a daily part of most people's morning, except for the very young. It is very finely ground (almost powdered) and sold in small quantities to retain freshness. It is also usually served in small portions, in demitasse or espresso cups, with a lot of sugar.

You can best approximate the taste of Cuban coffee by using finely ground Jamaican beans. If you prefer milk in your coffee, see the recipe on the following page. Cuban-Americans also enjoy their coffee with generous amounts of sugar. I have added sugar to all the coffee recipes since that is how it is typically made, but if you wish to omit the sugar, that's fine.

2 cups water
2 tablespoons finely ground coffee
Sugar to taste

Make the coffee using the method you prefer. Pour into espresso or demitasse cups, add sugar to taste, and serve.

CUBAN COFFEE WITH MILK
Café con Leche

Makes 3 servings

In Cuba, *café con leche* is generally served only at breakfast time and is sometimes followed by *café puro* (espresso). However, many people in the United States prefer its milky, milder taste to straight Cuban coffee and consume it throughout the day.

2 cups water
2 tablespoons finely ground coffee
2 cups milk
Sugar to taste (optional)

Make the coffee using the method you prefer. While the coffee is brewing, warm the milk in a small saucepan over low heat. Pour the coffee into regular-size coffee cups, filling about halfway. Add the warm milk to the cups. Add sugar to taste, and serve.

ICED CUBAN COFFEE
Café Helado

Makes 3 servings

On a sultry afternoon, no other beverage is quite as stimulating as a tall glass of iced coffee. A dollop of fresh whipped cream on top adds a special touch if you're serving it to guests with a light mid-afternoon snack. If you prefer not to whip the cream, it may be added in liquid form to the coffee.

2 cups water
2 tablespoons finely ground coffee
¼ cup heavy cream

1 teaspoon sugar
Crushed ice
Sugar to taste (optional)

Make the coffee using the method you prefer. Allow to cool slightly while whipping the cream. In a small bowl with an electric mixer, whip the cream until stiff, then mix in the 1 teaspoon sugar.

Fill tall glasses with crushed ice. Pour the cooled coffee evenly into the glasses. Add sugar to taste. Top each glass with a large dollop of whipped cream, and serve.

HOT CHOCOLATE COFFEE
Café con Chocolate Caliente

Makes 4 servings

Coffee and chocolate are two tastes that blend together superbly. This hot chocolate coffee is lovely after dinner, with or instead of dessert.

2 squares semisweet chocolate
1 cup Cuban coffee (made with
   1 cup water and 1 tablespoon finely ground coffee)
3 tablespoons plus 1 teaspoon
   sugar

¼ cup heavy cream
2 cups milk
Dark chocolate shavings for
   garnish

Melt the chocolate with the coffee and 3 tablespoons of the sugar in the top of a double boiler, over medium-high heat. Meanwhile, in a small mixing bowl with an electric mixer, whip the cream until stiff. Add the remaining 1 teaspoon sugar and mix.

When the chocolate and sugar are melted in the coffee, blend together and whisk in the milk. When the coffee mixture is hot but not boiling, pour into 4 coffee cups and top with dollops of whipped cream. Sprinkle chocolate shavings on top, and serve.

RUM-SPIKED COFFEE
Café con Ron

Makes 4 servings

Spiked coffee topped with fresh whipped cream is a spirited beverage to serve after a dinner party. You may substitute a coffee liqueur, such as Tía María or Kahlúa, or a chocolate liqueur for the rum, if you wish. (Add less sugar if you use a sweet liqueur.)

¼ cup heavy cream
1 teaspoon plus 3 tablespoons
*   sugar*
2 cups Cuban coffee (made with
*   2 cups water and 2 table-*
*   spoons finely ground coffee)*

4½ ounces (3 jiggers) dark
*   rum*

In a small mixing bowl with an electric mixer, whip the cream until stiff. Mix in 1 teaspoon of the sugar.

When the coffee is just finished brewing and still very hot, stir in the rum and the remaining 3 tablespoons sugar. When the sugar is dissolved, pour into 4 coffee cups. Top with spoonfuls of whipped cream, and serve.

PAPAYA-BANANA BATIDO
Batido de Plátano y Papaya

Makes 1 large drink

This fruit shake is sheer nectar: naturally sweet, thick, and delicious. Check page 24 before handling the papaya and use a ripe, brown banana.

1 cup peeled, seeded, and diced
  ripe papaya (page 24)
½ cup diced ripe banana

1 cup milk
½ cup crushed ice

In a blender, puree the papaya, banana, milk, and crushed ice. Pour into a tall glass and serve immediately.

GUAVA BATIDO
Batido de Guayaba

Makes 1 large drink

Guavas, which are indigenous to Cuba, are sold in the fruit markets of Little Havana. This recipe uses canned or bottled guava puree, which is widely available in Hispanic markets, health food stores, and many supermarkets—in both sweetened and unsweetened form.

½ cup unsweetened guava puree
  (see headnote)
1 cup milk

3 tablespoons sugar
½ cup crushed ice

Place the guava puree and milk in a blender. Add the sugar and ice and blend until smooth. Pour into a tall glass and serve.

PAPAYA-MANGO BATIDO
Batido de Mango y Papaya

Makes 3 servings

The papaya and mango combine to make this an especially sweet, lush nectar. Since this drink contains ice that melts and the blending of the ingredients is a temporary emulsion, it should be made to order.

1½ cups milk
1 cup diced mango (page 23)

1 cup diced papaya (page 24)
½ cup crushed ice

In a blender, puree the milk, mango, papaya, and ice until smooth. Pour into 3 tall glasses and serve.

SPICED CALYPSO PUNCH
Ponche Calypso

Makes 6–8 servings

This is a festive nonalcoholic punch to serve to children and teetotaling guests at a party. You can dress it up with slices of fresh fruit.

2 cups orange juice
1½ cups pineapple juice
¼ cup lime juice
1 cup boiling water
¼ cup honey
¼ teaspoon nutmeg

¼ teaspoon cinnamon
6 whole cloves
1½ cups ginger ale
Lime wedges for garnish
Crushed ice

In a large punch bowl, mix the orange juice, pineapple juice, and lime juice. In a small mixing bowl, mix the boiling water with the honey, nutmeg, cinnamon, and cloves. Set aside to cool.

Remove the cloves from the honey and spice mixture and discard. Add the mixture to the punchbowl. Add the ginger ale and stir. Garnish with lemon wedges and serve in glasses over crushed ice.

COCONUT MILK
Leche de Coco

Makes approximately 4½ cups

Coconut milk is actually the meat of the coconut pureed with hot water. Once chilled, it can be used to make fresh Piña Coladas (page 292) and other cocktails, or drunk straight over ice. Use a green coconut, which will be juicier.

Meat of 1 green coconut, chopped   *1 cup hot water*
  (page 20)   *3 cups boiling water*

In a blender, puree the coconut meat with 1 cup hot water. When liquefied, pour into a bowl and add the boiling water. Let stand 30 minutes.

   Strain the liquid over a bowl, discarding the solids. Chill in the refrigerator. Pour over crushed ice and serve, or use in a cocktail.

COCONUT WATER
Agua de Coco

Yields ½ to 1 cup (depending on size of coconut)

Coconut water has been called "the nectar of the gods" because of its pure, sweet taste. Only immature, green coconuts yield coconut water, since the meat of the mature fruit dries up.

1 green coconut (page 20)

Using a small hammer and a clean nail or an icepick, pierce the eyes of the coconut. Drain the liquid into a bowl. Pour into a glass over crushed ice and serve, or use in a cocktail.

CUBA LIBRE

Makes 1 serving

This simple mixed drink has a very significant name; it means "Free Cuba!" It is very popular in Miami as well as in Cuba.

Ice cubes
1½ ounces (1 jigger) light rum
3 ounces (2 jiggers) cola

Juice from 1 lime wedge
1 lime wedge for garnish

Fill a tall glass three quarters full with ice cubes. Add the rum, cola, and lime juice. Stir together, garnish with a lime wedge, and serve.

PRESIDENTE

Makes 1 serving

This drink is as strong as the Cuban president for whom it was named: General Menocal, who had a taste for strong cocktails as well as power.

Ice cubes
¼ ounce (1½ teaspoons) dry
  vermouth
¾ ounce (½ jigger) sweet
  vermouth

1½ ounces (1 jigger) white rum
Splash of grenadine
1 maraschino cherry for garnish

Fill a short cocktail glass with ice cubes. Pour in the dry vermouth, sweet vermouth, and rum. Stir well. Add a splash of grenadine and a maraschino cherry, and serve.

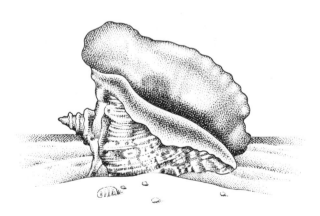

MOJITO

Makes 1 serving

Ernest Hemingway, who was famous for his prodigious drinking as well as his writing, had a saying: "My Daiquiri at the Floridita, my Mojito at the Bodeguita." He was referring to his two favorite watering holes in Havana: La Bodeguita del Medio Restaurant and the Floridita Restaurant. Both establishments are still going strong and Mojitos continue to be one of the most popular cocktails in Cuba.

Juice of ½ lime
1 teaspoon fine granulated sugar
Crushed ice
2 ounces (1⅓ jiggers) white
   rum

Splash of club soda
1 large mint sprig for garnish

Stir the lime juice and sugar together in a tall glass until the sugar dissolves. Fill the glass three quarters full with crushed ice. Add the rum and a splash of club soda, and stir well. Add the mint sprig, and serve.

RUM COCKTAIL
Coctel de Ron

Makes 1 serving

This drink allows the true taste of the rum to come through, without being overwhelmed by juices or liqueurs. Bacardi light rum, which has been produced in Puerto Rico since the Cuban Revolution, is favored by many rum connoisseurs. Add a dash of maraschino cherry juice as a sweetener, if you wish.

Crushed ice
1½ ounces (1 jigger) light rum
2 tablespoons lime juice

Splash of maraschino cherry juice (optional)
1 maraschino cherry for garnish

In a tall glass three quarters filled with crushed ice, mix the rum and lime juice. Add a splash of maraschino cherry juice, if desired. Top with a cherry, and serve.

CUBAN COCKTAIL
Coctel Cubano

Makes 1 serving

Light rum blends harmoniously with sweet, fruity brandies, such as the apricot brandy used in this cocktail.

Crushed ice
2 ounces (1⅓ jiggers) light
   rum

¾ ounce (½ jigger) apricot
   brandy
1 tablespoon lime juice

Fill a tall glass three quarters full with ice cubes and pour in the rum, brandy, and lime juice. Mix well and serve.

Another way to serve a Cuban cocktail is to pour all ingredients into a cocktail shaker, mix by shaking well, and strain into a short cocktail glass three quarters filled with crushed ice, with a twist of lime.

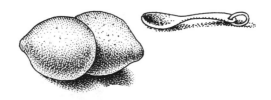

CUBAN SPECIAL
Cubano Especial

Makes 1 serving

This drink features Curaçao, which comes from the Dutch Caribbean island of the same name. It is an orange liqueur made from the bitter oranges that flourish on the island.

Ice cubes
2 ounces (1⅓ jiggers) light rum
1 teaspoon Curaçao
1 tablespoon pineapple juice

1 tablespoon lime juice
1 maraschino cherry and 1
* pineapple chunk on a cock-*
* tail stick for garnish (optional)*

Fill a tall glass three quarters full with ice cubes. Add the rum, Curaçao, pineapple juice, and lime juice, and mix well. Garnish with the maraschino cherry and pineapple chunk on a swizzle stick, if desired.

Another way to serve a Cuban Special is to shake all ingredients (except the garnish) in a cocktail shaker. Strain into an Old-Fashioned or Whiskey Sour glass, garnish if desired, and serve.

RUM SWIZZLE

Makes 1 serving

This drink was a favorite of the tourists who flocked to Havana in the 1950s. It includes Angostura bitters, a Trinidadian flavoring that is used in many Caribbean cocktails.

Ice cubes
1 tablespoon lime juice
1½ ounces (1 jigger) dark rum

Dash of Angostura bitters
Club soda
1 lime wedge for garnish

In a tall glass filled three quarters full with ice, stir together the lime juice, rum, and bitters. Add club soda until the glass is full, and mix well. Garnish with a lime wedge, and serve.

SUPER RUM SWIZZLE

Makes 1 serving

This stronger version of the rum swizzle features dark rum, which was the original variety of rum produced in the Caribbean. It was notorious for its potency and unsavory association with pirates.

1 cup crushed ice
1½ ounces (1 jigger) dark rum
1 tablespoon lime juice

2 dashes of Angostura bitters
Twist of lime for garnish

In a cocktail shaker, shake together the crushed ice, rum, lime juice, and bitters. Strain into an Old-Fashioned or Whiskey Sour glass, three quarters filled with crushed ice. Garnish with a lime twist, and serve.

LIME DAIQUIRI
Daiquirí de Lima

Makes 1 serving

The Daiquiri was invented by an American mining engineer named Jennings Cox, who supervised copper mines in eastern Cuba, outside the small town of Daiquirí. In 1896, Jennings unexpectedly received guests from the United States. He was out of gin and was afraid that the Americans would not care for the local Cuban rum. To improve and disguise its taste, he added lime juice and sugar and chilled the concoction. When he served it to his guests, it was a big hit, and so the Daiquiri was born.

Two years later, during the Spanish-American War, Jennings Cox brought his creation to an American general and his men, who had landed on the beach at Daiquirí. The navy officers later introduced "Daiquiris" at the Army and Navy Club in Washington, D.C., thereby launching the drink's popularity in this country.

1 cup crushed ice
2 tablespoons lime juice
1 teaspoon sugar

1½ ounces (1 jigger) light rum
Lime twist for garnish

In a cocktail shaker, combine the crushed ice, lime juice, sugar, and rum. Shake vigorously until well blended and chilled. Strain into a Whiskey Sour or Old-Fashioned glass, garnish with a lime twist, and serve.

MANGO DAIQUIRI
Daiquirí de Mango

Makes 2 servings

This recipe combines Curaçao and mango to create a heady ambrosia. The chunks of mango you will have left over from the cocktail can be used as an exotic garnish.

4 ounces (2⅓ jiggers) light rum
1 ounce (⅔ jigger) Curaçao
½ cup chopped mango (page 23)

2 tablespoons lime juice
1 tablespoon sugar
2 cups crushed ice
Mango chunks for garnish

In a blender, combine the rum, Curaçao, mango, lime juice, sugar, and ice. Blend until smooth. Pour into 2 Daiquiri glasses or large champagne glasses. Garnish each drink with mango chunks skewered on a cocktail stick, and serve.

PEACH DAIQUIRI
Daiquirí de Melocotón

Makes 1 serving

Peaches originated in China, and were spread throughout Europe by the Romans. Later, the Spaniards introduced them to the New World lands they colonized. Peach Daiquiris should be made with ripe peaches, which are yielding when pressed. If you wish to hasten the ripening of unripe peaches, place them in a brown paper bag with the top folded down for 2 to 3 days in a dry, warm place.

2 ounces (1⅓ jiggers) light rum
½ medium peach, peeled, pitted, and chopped
1 tablespoon sugar
1 cup crushed ice
1 peach slice for garnish

In a blender, combine the rum, peach, sugar, and ice. Blend until smooth. Pour into a Daiquiri glass or large champagne glass. Garnish with a slice of peach on the rim, and serve with a straw.

PINEAPPLE DAIQUIRI
Daiquirí de Piña

Makes 1 serving

This recipe calls for Cointreau, which is a superb but very expensive liqueur. Triple Sec or another orange liqueur may be substituted, if you wish.

2 ounces (1½ jiggers) light
  rum
1 tablespoon Cointreau
½ cup crushed pineapple
1 tablespoon lime juice

1 tablespoon sugar or to taste
½ cup crushed ice
1 pineapple slice for garnish
  (optional)

In a blender, combine the rum, Cointreau, crushed pineapple, lime juice, sugar, and crushed ice. Blend until smooth, taste, and add more ice or sugar if desired. Pour into a Daiquiri glass or a large champagne glass. Garnish with a piece of fresh pineapple if desired, and serve with a straw.

BANANA DAIQUIRI
Daiquirí de Plátano

Makes 1 serving

Bananas make especially thick, creamy Daiquiris. These delectable drinks, which were invented in Cuba, are now served at beach resorts throughout the world.

1½ ounces (1 jigger) light rum
1 tablespoon Triple Sec
½ ripe banana, cut into 6 pieces
1 tablespoon lemon juice
1 cup crushed ice
Twist of lemon for garnish

In a blender, blend the rum, Triple Sec, banana, lemon juice, and ice until smooth. Pour into a large champagne glass or a Daiquiri glass, garnish with a twist of lemon, and serve with a straw.

PIÑA COLADA

Makes 1 serving

Piña Coladas (literally, "strained pineapple") served in coconut shells, with umbrellas and fancy garnishes, are a silly but fun tourist attraction at many beach resort bars. Usually, Piña Coladas are made with canned coconut cream, but I prefer the cleaner taste of fresh coconut milk.

1½ ounces (1 jigger) light
rum
1 ounce (⅔ jigger) chilled Coco-
nut Milk (page 278)
¼ cup crushed pineapple

1 tablespoon lime juice
½ cup crushed ice
1 maraschino cherry and 1
pineapple chunk for garnish

In a blender, combine the rum, coconut milk, crushed pineapple, lime juice, and crushed ice. Blend until smooth. Pour into a large wineglass or a tall glass. Spear a cherry and pineapple chunk on a cocktail stick, add to the glass, and serve.

YELLOW BIRD

Makes 1 serving

The Yellow Bird is a heady cocktail that gets its name and its sunny color from Galliano, a golden, anise-flavored Italian liqueur.

1 cup crushed ice
1½ ounces (1 jigger) dark rum
1 tablespoon Galliano

1 tablespoon Triple Sec
2 tablespoons lemon juice
Lemon twist for garnish

In a cocktail shaker, vigorously shake together the crushed ice, rum, Galliano, Triple Sec, and lemon juice. Strain into an Old-Fashioned or Whiskey Sour glass, garnish with a lemon twist, and serve.

RUM AND COCONUT WATER
Agua de Coco con Ron

Makes 1 serving

Colonial Cubans drank rum and coconut juice long before more complicated cocktails were invented for tourists. And this is still one of the most popular ways for the natives to imbibe their rum.

Ice cubes
1½ ounces (1 jigger) light rum
Coconut Water freshly drained
  from 1 green coconut (page
  20)

Lime twist for garnish

Fill a tall glass with ice cubes. Pour in the rum and coconut water. Stir, garnish with a lime twist, and serve.

COLD RUM TODDY
Ponche de Ron Frío

Makes 1 serving

There are hundreds of varieties of rum produced in the Caribbean, from dry, mild light rums to heavy dark rums that are aged in charred oak casks for up to 25 years. Here is a way to savor a full-bodied dark rum with a pungent bouquet.

1 teaspoon superfine sugar   Ice cubes
¼ cup club soda   Lemon twist for garnish
1½ ounces (1 jigger) dark rum

In an Old-Fashioned glass, dissolve the sugar in the club soda. Add the rum and enough ice cubes to fill the glass. Stir, garnish with lemon, and serve.

HOT RUM TODDY
Ponche de Ron Caliente con Mantequilla

Makes 1 serving

Hot Rum Toddies have a reputation for being restorative when people are feeling ill. Whether this is valid or not is disputable, but the warm rum certainly has a soothing effect.

In 1892, a court doctor prescribed Cuban rum made by the Bacardi family for a sickly young Spanish royal prince. The prince's health improved and after he became the King of Spain he granted the Bacardis the right to display the Spanish coat of arms on their labels.

1 teaspoon superfine sugar
¾ cup boiling water
1½ ounces (1 jigger) dark rum
1 teaspoon butter

1 dash of Angostura bitters
1 dash each of nutmeg and
cinnamon

In an Old-Fashioned glass (heat-proof, so the boiling water doesn't crack the glass), dissolve the sugar with ½ cup of the boiling water. Add the rum, butter, and bitters, and the remaining ¼ cup water if needed to fill glass. Sprinkle with nutmeg and cinnamon on top, and serve warm.

RUM PUNCH
Ponche de Ron

Makes 1 serving

This sunny, refreshing punch combines a medley of tart juices with a splash of sweet grenadine.

Ice cubes
1 ounce (2 tablespoons) lime
  juice
1 ounce (⅔ jigger) orange juice

1 ounce (⅔ jigger) pineapple juice
1 teaspoon grenadine
2 ounces (1⅓ jiggers) light rum
1 lime wedge for garnish

Into a tall glass three quarters filled with ice cubes, pour the lime juice, orange juice, pineapple juice, grenadine, and rum. Stir, garnish with lime wedge, and serve.

PLANTER'S PUNCH

Makes 1 serving

Contrary to common belief, planter's punch is not a specific recipe; it can be any drink made of rum and fruit juice. In the days of the great sugar plantations in Cuba, certain plantations had their own unique ancestral recipes for planter's punch, which were proudly passed down through the generations.

1½ ounces (1 jigger) dark
  rum
1½ ounces (1 jigger) orange
  juice

1 teaspoon lime juice
½ teaspoon grenadine
Ice cubes
1 maraschino cherry for garnish

Combine the rum, orange juice, lime juice, and grenadine in a cocktail shaker. Shake vigorously and pour into a tall glass filled with ice cubes. Top with a cherry, and serve.

MILK PUNCH
Ponche de Leche

Makes 1 serving

Wealthy Cuban planters often had pocket-size silver nutmeg graters to powder fresh nutmeg for their rum punches. This milk punch is a rich, elegant dessert drink.

2 ounces (1⅓ jiggers) dark rum
2 ounces (¼ cup, or 1⅓ jiggers) milk
½ cup crushed ice

Dash of Angostura bitters
1 teaspoon sugar
Pinch of ground nutmeg

In a cocktail shaker, combine the rum, milk, ice, bitters, and sugar. Shake until blended. Pour unstrained into a short glass. Sprinkle with nutmeg and serve.

SANGRÍA

Makes 6–8 servings

This refreshing wine–fruit punch is a Spanish tradition. Now Sangría is in vogue in Miami, where it is a popular choice in Cuban restaurants.

1 bottle full-bodied Spanish red wine
1 cup club soda
1 orange, thinly sliced
1 lemon, thinly sliced

1 apple, cored and cut into ⅛-inch pieces
1 peach, pitted and cut into ⅛-inch pieces

In a large pitcher, combine the wine with the club soda. Stir in the orange, lemon, apple, and peach. Serve chilled in large wineglasses filled with ice.

A HOLIDAY FEAST

Cubanuban-Americans are talented at the art of celebration. They often host lavish dinners to celebrate birthdays, saints' days, weddings, anniversaries, Epiphany, Easter, and Christmas. Christmas is the most important holiday for Cuban-Americans, a time when they carry on the tradition of gathering with family and friends for a bountiful feast.

Here is a menu for a traditional Cuban feast that will serve at least 10 people. (There will be leftovers of the suckling pig and other dishes.) Of course, you may add or omit any foods that you wish. The only requirement is that you enjoy your feast with people you love, in quintessential Cuban-American fashion.

MENU

- Rum cocktails of your choice (see Beverages chapter)
- Fruit Salad with Lemon-Lime Dressing: double all ingredients (page 46)
- Traditional Black Bean Soup: double all ingredients (page 56)
- A hearty red wine of your choice
- Roast Suckling Pig (page 302)
- Orange-Raisin Cornmeal Stuffing (page 306)
- Roasted Boniatos (page 304)
- Roasted Sweet Onions (page 305)
- Yuca with Garlic Sauce: double all ingredients (page 78)
- Paella (page 308)
- Sautéed Butter-Rum Plantains (page 307)
- Cuban Coffee and Rum-Spiked Coffee: increase amounts as needed (pages 269 and 273)
- Traditional Flan: double all ingredients—use two dishes (page 242)
- Rum Rice Pudding (page 310)

ROAST SUCKLING PIG
Lechón Asado

Makes over 10 servings

Roast suckling pig is the traditional centerpiece of Cuban Christmas dinners. In Cuba, enormous suckling pigs are often roasted on spits over open fires. While this gives the pig a wonderful flavor, it is impractical for most people in this country, so this recipe will tell you how to roast a relatively small suckling pig in your oven.

The ingredient that gives Cuban-style suckling pig its special favor is bitter orange (page 18). Lemon, lime, or orange juice can be substituted in this recipe, but bitter orange will give the pig a distinct and superior flavor.

Suckling pig is available at most butcher shops, but you should go to your butcher at least 2 weeks in advance to order your pig. Ask your butcher to dress the pig and to remove the eyeballs and lower lids. The dressed pig should weigh 10 to 12 pounds.

1 10–12 pound dressed, oven-ready suckling pig
2 tablespoons salt
1 medium onion, minced
½ cup melted butter
½ cup bitter orange juice
8 garlic cloves, minced
Freshly ground black pepper
Orange-Raisin Cornmeal Stuffing (page 306)

1 cup hot soup stock or water, mixed with ½ cup melted butter and ½ cup bitter orange juice, for basting if needed
Watercress or green-leaf lettuce for dressing platter
Parsley sprigs for forming wreath around neck
1 apple, lemon, or lime for mouth
Cranberries or raisins for eyes

Wash clean the prepared pig and pat dry with paper towels. Sprinkle the pig inside and out with salt and place in a large roasting pan.

In a small bowl, combine the onion, melted butter, bitter orange juice, and garlic. Liberally brush the pig inside and out with the mixture until it is used up. Sprinkle the pig with freshly ground black pepper. Refrigerate overnight.

Preheat the oven to 450°F. Remove the pig from the refrigerator and stuff loosely with the stuffing. Close up the opening with skewers and tie with kitchen string. Place the pig belly side down in the roasting pan. Place either a piece of wood or a ball of aluminum foil about the size of a large lemon in the pig's mouth to keep it open. Skewer the legs into position by pulling the forelegs forward and bending the hind legs into a crouching position. Cover the tail and ears with aluminum foil to prevent burning.

Place the pig in the oven and baste after 15 minutes. Reduce the heat to 325°F. and roast 3 to 4 hours, 20 minutes for each pound, basting every 15 minutes with the pan juices. If there are not enough pan juices to easily baste the pig, prepare the soup stock mixture to baste with.

To test if the pig is done, prick the thigh with a fork or the tip of a small knife. When the juices run clear, not pink, and the meat is tender, the pig is finished.

Remove from the oven and allow to sit 10 minutes. Meanwhile, place a bed of watercress or green-leaf lettuce on a very large serving platter. Twist a wreath for the pig's neck with the parsley sprigs. If desired, arrange Roasted Boniatos and Roasted Sweet Onions around periphery of platter (recipes follow in this chapter).

Remove the foil from the pig's tail and ears. Transfer the pig to the platter and place the parsley wreath around its neck. Remove the foil or wood from the mouth and replace with a lemon, lime, or apple. Place the raisins or cranberries in the eyes. Carve at the table.

ROASTED BONIATOS
Boniatos Asados

Makes 10 servings

The boniatos will absorb some of the flavor and aroma of the suckling pig if they are roasted in the same pan. You can arrange them with other accompaniments around the pig on a very large platter or serve them alongside in a separate dish.

5 large boniatos (page 18)
1 tablespoon melted butter

Wash and scrub the boniatos, then pat dry with paper towel. Brush the boniatos lightly with the melted butter.

When the suckling pig has 1 hour and 45 minutes of roasting time left, place the boniatos alongside the pig in the roasting pan. After the boniatos have baked 1 hour, pierce them in a few spots with a fork to allow steam to escape. Bake 45 minutes longer, then remove from the oven. Transfer the boniatos to the serving platter with the pig or to a separate serving dish. Cut the boniatos in half when serving.

ROASTED SWEET ONIONS
Cebollas Asadas

Makes 10 servings

Sweet onions can add a final touch to the spectacular presentation of the suckling pig. They also meld with the other accompaniments to create a pungent aroma that will kindle your guests' appetites.

5 medium onions, root end
sliced off
1 tablespoon melted butter

When the suckling pig has 1½ hours of roasting time remaining, add the onions to the roasting pan alongside the pig and brush them lightly with melted butter. Bake 1½ hours, then remove from the oven and transfer to the serving platter with the pig. Squeeze the onions so the middle core comes out. Remove and discard the outer skins. Cut the onions in half when serving.

ORANGE-RAISIN CORNMEAL STUFFING

Makes over 10 servings

In this recipe, the orange zest adds a citrusy tang that offsets the sweetness of the raisins. Use cornbread that is slightly stale, or has been left to dry out in the open air for 1 to 2 hours. This special recipe uses ingredients not normally found in American stuffing.

6 cups stale cornbread (page 231), cut into ¼-inch pieces
1 cup seedless raisins
½ cup butter
½ cup chopped onion
4 cloves garlic, minced
1 cup chopped celery
1 tablespoon grated orange zest
1 teaspoon salt
½ teaspoon ground cumin
2 tablespoons chopped fresh cilantro

In a large mixing bowl, combine the bread cubes and raisins, and set aside. Over medium heat, melt the butter in a medium-size sauté pan. Add the onions, garlic, and celery, and sauté until tender, about 4 to 6 minutes.

Remove from the heat and pour the vegetable mixture over the bread and raisins. Toss until well mixed. Add the orange zest, salt, cumin, and cilantro. Toss until all the ingredients are blended.

SAUTÉED BUTTER-RUM PLANTAINS
Plátanos Dulces en Mantequilla y Ron

Makes 10 servings

No Cuban feast is complete without sweet plantains. In this festive recipe, the plantains are enlivened with brown sugar and dark rum. Serve as a side dish with the suckling pig.

½ cup butter
6 large, ripe plantains, peeled
  and sliced diagonally into
  1-inch pieces (page 25)

¼ cup dark brown sugar
¼ cup dark rum

In a large sauté pan, melt the butter over medium heat. Add the plantain slices and fry about 4 minutes on each side. (Fry in 2 batches if the pan is not large enough to spread evenly in a single layer.) Remove the plantains from the pan with a slotted spoon and place on a large, warm platter.

Add the sugar and rum to the pan and stir until the mixture is bubbly hot and slightly thickened, approximately 6 to 8 minutes. Add the plantains to the rum mixture and stir together. Transfer the mixture to the warm platter.

PAELLA

Makes 10 servings

Paella is a classic Spanish dish which became popular in Cuba when it was colonized by the Spaniards. It is named for the cooking vessel in which it is traditionally prepared, called a paellero. If you do not own a paellero, you can use a large, lidded casserole. You can prepare the paella while the suckling pig is roasting, and serve it after the pig is presented. For this recipe, it's best to buy link Spanish sausage (chorizo) from your butcher instead of bulk sausage, and use Valencia rice. Paella is time-consuming and has many special ingredients, but this is part of what makes it a very festive dish.

½ cup olive oil
1 2-pound broiling or frying chicken, cut into 6–8 serving pieces
½ cup diced ham
½ cup cooked Spanish sausage (page 144), sliced into ½-inch pieces
¼ cup diced onion,
4 garlic cloves, minced
2 large tomatoes, peeled, seeded, and coarsely chopped
1½ pounds medium raw shrimp, peeled and deveined (page 27)

1 dozen littleneck clams, with shells scrubbed
1 teaspoon salt
2 cups Valencia rice
4 cups boiling water
1 cup green peas, fresh or frozen
¼ cup minced fresh parsley
5 saffron threads, or more to taste
3 red bell peppers, seeded, deribbed, cut into quarters lengthwise, and roasted (page 25)
1 rock lobster tail, cooked, meat cut into ½-inch pieces

Preheat the oven to 350°F. In a paellero or large casserole, heat the olive oil over medium-high heat. Add the chicken and cook 10 minutes, turning to brown all sides. Remove the chicken to a platter lined with paper towels, and set aside.

Add the ham, sausage, onion, garlic, and tomatoes to the

paellero and cook until heated through. Add the shrimp, clams, and salt, cover, and cook 5 minutes. Remove the clams and shrimp to a platter and cover with aluminum foil.

Stir the rice, water, peas, parsley, and saffron into the paellero. Add the chicken to the rice mixture, cover, reduce the heat to medium-low, and simmer 20 minutes, until the rice is tender. When the rice is finished, mix in the roasted peppers. Arrange the chicken pieces so they are mostly on top. Cover and bake for 15 minutes.

Remove the paella from the oven and add the shrimp, clams, and lobster. Mix well, cover, and bake another 5 minutes, until heated through. Serve hot.

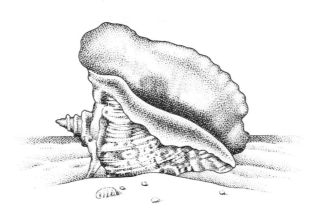

RUM RICE PUDDING
Pudín de Arroz con Ron

Makes 10 servings

This delicious rum rice pudding is a perfect finale for your feast. You can make it ahead of time, chill it in the refrigerator, and serve it cold, or you can bake it while your guests are enjoying their main course and serve it warm. Complement the pudding with Cuban coffee, spiked with rum if desired, and present it along with the flan for dessert. Your guests may be satisfied from the other dishes, but they will probably succumb to these irresistible temptations.

¼ cup light rum
5 cups cooked long-grain white
   rice (page 95)
⅔ cup light brown sugar
⅔ cup raisins

10 large eggs, beaten
4 cups milk
1 teaspoon salt
2 teaspoons lemon juice
Butter for greasing baking dish

Preheat the oven to 350°F. In a large mixing bowl, combine the rum, rice, brown sugar, raisins, eggs, milk, salt, and lemon juice. Grease two 8-inch round baking dishes with butter. Divide the rice mixture evenly between the baking dishes and bake 40 to 50 minutes, until set. Chill in the refrigerator and serve cold, or serve immediately.

INDEX

Achiote
  Oil, 120
  seeds, notes on, 120
Ajiaco, 83
Almond(s)
  Cookies, 253
  Flan, Country-Baked, 245
  Pan-Fried Grouper with, 191
  -Raisin Bread, 226
  Syrup, Fried Yuca Dough with, 252
Appetizers
  Conch Fritters with Cilantro
    Dipping Sauce, 44
  Crab Cakes, Spicy, with Papaya
    Chutney, 40
  Escabeche, 39
  Fresh Corn and Red Pepper
    Tamales, 84
  Fruit Salad with Lemon-Lime
    Dressing, 46
  Meat-and-Onion-Stuffed Turn-
    overs, 130
  Pasteles, 132
  Pork Tamales, 150
  Sausage Empanadas with Pi-
    miento Salsa, 34
  Shrimp
    Breaded, with Tomato-Caper
      Salsa, 204
    Fried, with Coconut-Beer Batter
      and Orange Cocktail Sauce,
      42
    in Garlic Wine Sauce, 33
    Sweet Rum, 38
  see also Croquettes
Avocado(s)
  Cucumber, and Soup, Cold, 62

Avocoado(s) (cont'd)
  notes on, 90
  with Vinaigrette, 90

Baby Back Ribs with Spicy Papaya
  Sauce, 143
Bacon Dressing, Tri-Colored Bean
  Salad with, 106
Baked Rum-Raisin Pudding, 248
Baked Salt Cod, 193
Baked Yuca Stuffed with Shredded
  Beef, 124
Banana(s)
  Custard, Frozen, 259
  Daiquiri, 291
  Fresh Coconut and, Cream Pie, 254
  in Fruit Salad with Lemon-Lime
    Dressing, 46
  Papaya-, Batido, 274
Batido(s)
  Guava, 275
  Papaya
    -Banana, 274
    -Mango, 276
Bean(s)
  black
    Chili, 111
    Flan, 110
    Honey-Rum-Baked, 108
    leftover, notes on, 96
    notes on, 17
    recipe for, 96
    and Rice, 98
    and Rice, Rum-Flavored, 101
    Salad, Marinated, 102
    Sauce, Peppered, Roast Pork
      with, 146

Bean(s), black *(cont'd)*
  Sauce, Shrimp with, 211
  Soup, Traditional, 56
  Spicy, wth Tomatoes, Onions,
    and Peppers, 103
  -Steamed Snapper, 194
  in Tri-Colored Bean Salad with
    Bacon Dressing, 106
  notes on, 93
  red
    kidney, *in* Tri-Colored Bean
      Salad with Bacon Dressing,
      106
    notes on, 18
    and Rice, 104
    Soup, 67
  Salad, Tri-Colored, with Bacon
    Dressing, 106
  to soak, 18
  string, *in* Tri-Colored Bean Salad
    with Bacon Dressing, 106
  white
    in Galician Potage, 61
    kidney, notes on, 18
    and Pork, Baked, Sweet, 105
    and Tomato Soup, 64
Beef
  in Ajiaco, 83
  Cuban Pot Roast, 126
  ground
    in Black Bean Chili, 111
    in Picadillo, 121
    in Spicy Stuffed Peppers with
      Tomato Sauce, 128
    in Tamale Pie with Sweet and
      Spicy Meat Filling, 127
  Oxtail Stew, 122
  in Pasteles, 132
  in Ropa Vieja, 119
  Shredded, Baked Yuca Stuffed
    with, 124
  Steak(s)
    Flank, with Port Wine Mari-
      nade, 134
    Palomilla, 123
    Rolled Stuffed, 135
  Stock, 54

Beer, Coconut-, Batter and Orange
  Cocktail Sauce, Fried
  Shrimp with, 42
Beverages
  Coconut
    Milk, 278
    Water, 279
    Water, Rum and, 293
  Cuba Libre, 280
  Rum
    Swizzle, 286
    toddies. *See* Rum
  see also Batidos; Cocktails; Coffee;
    Punches
Bitter oranges. *See* Oranges
Black beans. *See* Beans
Black pepper, notes on, 25
Boniato(s)
  to bake or boil, 81
  Chips, 80
  Dumplings, 81
  notes on, 18, 73
  Roasted, 304
  Rum-Glazed, 82
Braised Loin of Pork with Papaya, 141
Bread(s)
  Almond-Raisin, 226
  Cassava, 217
    Rolls, 222
  Cheese, 221
  Churros, 229
  Cornmeal, 231
  Cuban, 218
  to freeze, 215
  Orange, 227
  Papaya and Raisin, 225
  Plantain, Sweet, 224
  Tomato-Pimiento, 220
  see also Cornbread; Muffins
Breaded Shrimp with Tomato-
  Caper Salsa, 204
Breast of chicken. *See* Chicken
  breasts
Broiled Dolphin with Sweet Red Pep-
  per and Papaya Chutney, 198
Butter
  to clarify, 89

Butter *(cont'd)*
Mango, 235
-Rum Plantains, Sautéed, 307

Cake(s), Sponge, with Rum, 256
Calabaza
to cut, 19
Fritters, 79
notes on, 19
Soup, Sweet and Spicy, 68
Caper(s)
notes on, 19, 178
Tomato(es)
Olives, and, Crispy Baked
Chicken with, 178
Salsa, Breaded Shrimp with, 204
Cassava
Bread, 217
Rolls, 222
see also Yuca
Cayenne pepper, notes on, 25
Cheese
Bread, 221
Vegetable and, Omelet, 88
Chicken
breast(s)
of, al Ajillo, 166
Coconut-Stuffed, with Light
Cream Sauce, 168
in Crispy Fried Marinated
Chicken, 180
in Pastel de Maíz, 182
in Spicy Chicken Sauté with
Vegetables and Papaya, 167
in Sweet and Spicy Cilantro
Chicken, 177
Cilantro, Sweet and Spicy, 177
Country, Baked, 170
Croquettes with Sautéed Onions
and Peppers, 172
Golden Baked, with Tomatoes,
Olives and Capers, 178
Grilled, Sofrito, 184
Marinated, Crispy Fried, 180
in Paella, 308
and Rice, 163
Soup, 66

Chicken and Rice *(cont'd)*
Stew, 164
Roasted
Garlic-Marinated, 181
with Papaya Glaze, 174
Sauté, Spicy, with Vegetables and
Papaya, 167
Stock, 52
Chili, Black Bean, 111
Chilies, green
Spicy Cornbread with, 228
notes on, 25
see also Peppers
Chilled Lentil Salad with Spicy
Vinaigrette, 107
Chilled Yuca Soup, 58
Chocolate, Hot, Coffee, 272
Chorizo
in Ajiaco, 83
in Black Bean Chili, 111
in Galician Potage, 61
notes on, 19, 34, 144
in Paella, 302
in Peppers Stuffed with Spanish
Sausage and Tomato, 86
recipe for, 144
in Sausage Empanadas with
Pimiento Salsa, 34
Chowder, Conch, 65
Churros, 229
Chutney(s)
Papaya, 41
Spicy Crab Cakes with, 40
Sweet Red Pepper and Papaya,
Broiled Dolphin in, 198
Cider-and-Mango-Roasted Ham, 145
Cilantro
Chicken, Sweet and Spicy, 177
Cream of Garlic Soup with, 59
Dipping Sauce, Conch Fritters
with, 44
notes on, 20
Tomato
and Onion, Snapper Grilled
with, 209
Vinaigrette, Plantain Cro-
quettes with, 36

Clams, *in* Paella, 308
Classic Rice Pudding, 249
Cocktail(s)
  Cuban, 284
  Cuban Special, 285
  Mojito, 282
  Piña Colada, 292
  Presidente, 281
  Rum, 283
  Super Rum Swizzle, 286
  Yellow Bird, 292
  see also Daiquiris
Coconut
  -Beer Batter and Orange Cocktail
    Sauce, Fried Shrimp with, 42
  Fresh, and Banana Cream Pie, 254
  to grate, 20
  Ice Cream, 260
  Milk, 278
  Muffins, 232
  notes on, 20
  to open, 20
  -Rum Flan, 244
  Sauce, Snapper in, 196
  -Stuffed Chicken Breasts with
    Light Cream Sauce, 168
  Water, 279
    Rum and, 293
Cod
  salt
    Baked, 193
    Island Style, 192
    to soak, 192
  in Seafood Stew, 202
Coffee
  Cuban, 269
    Iced, 271
    with Milk, 270
  Hot Chocolate, 272
  Rum-Spiked, 273
Cold Cucumber and Avocado Soup, 62
Cold Rum Toddy, 294
Conch
  Chowder, 65
  to clean, 21
  Fritters with Cilantro Dipping
    Sauce, 44

Conch (*cont'd*)
  Marinated, Salad, 201
  notes on, 21, 44
Cookies, Almond, 253
Corn
  in Ajiaco, 83
  Fresh, and Red Pepper Tamales,
    84
  husks
    notes on, 21, 150
    to reconstitute, 21
  in Pastel de Maíz, 182
  Shrimp, and Potato Soup, 63
Cornbread
  with Green Chilies, Spicy, 228
  Sweet, 230
Cornmeal
  Bread, 231
    see also Cornbread
  notes on, 22
  Pudding, Old-Fashioned, 250
  -and-Raisin-Stuffed Pork Chops,
    155
  Stuffing, Orange-Raisin, 306
Country-Baked Almond Flan, 245
Country Baked Chicken, 170
Crab(s)
  Cakes, Spicy, with Papaya Chutney,
    40
  to clean, 22
  land, notes on, 202
  notes on, 22
  in Seafood Stew, 202
  see also Crabmeat
Cream of Garlic Soup with Cilan-
  tro, 59
Cream Pie, Fresh Coconut and
  Banana, 254
Cream Sauce, Light, Coconut-Stuffed
  Chicken Breasts with, 168
Crispy Fried Marinated Chicken, 180
Croquettes
  Chicken, with Sautéed Onions
    and Peppers, 172
  Ham and Potato, Spicy, 148
  Plantain, with Tomato-Cilantro
    Vinaigrette, 36

Cuba Libre, 280
Cuban Bread, 218
Cuban-Chinese Roast Loin of Pork,
    158
Cuban Cocktail, 284
Cuban coffee. *See* Coffee
Cuban feast, menu for, 301
Cuban Pot Roast, 126
Cuban Special, 285
Cucumber and Avocado Soup, Cold,
    62
Custard(s)
  Banana, Frozen, 259
  Plantain, 246

Daiquiri(s)
  Banana, 291
  Lime, 287
  Mango, 288
  Peach, 289
  Pineapple, 290
Desserts
  Almond Cookies, 253
  Bacon from Heaven, 251
  Flaming Mango Sauce over
      Homemade Vanilla Ice
      Cream, 258
  Fresh Coconut and Banana
      Cream Pie, 254
  Fried Yuca Dough with Almond
      Syrup, 252
  Fruit Salad with Lemon-Lime
      Dressing, 46
  Plantain Custard, 246
  Rum Mousse, Frozen, 247
  Sponge Cakes with Rum, 256
  Yuca, Fried, with Almond Syrup,
      252
  see also Flans (sweet); Ice creams;
      Puddings
Diplomatic Pudding, 241
Dipping Sauce, Cilantro, Conch
    Fritters with, 44
Dolphin
  Broiled, with Sweet Red Pepper
      and Papaya Chutney, 198
  notes on, 198

Dolphin (*cont'd*)
  for pompano *in* Poached Pompano
      with Orange-Rum Sauce, 210
Dressing(s)
  Bacon, Tri-Colored Bean Salad
      with, 106
  Lemon-Lime, Fruit Salad with, 46
  Mayonnaise, 41
  see also Sauces; Vinaigrettes
Dumplings, Boniato, 81

Empanadas, Sausage, with Pi-
    miento Salsa, 34
Escabeche, 39

Feast, Cuban, menu for, 301
Fish
  to bone, 22
  notes on, 22
  to skin, 23
  Stock, 51
  see also names of fish
Flaming Mango Sauce over Home-
    made Vanilla Ice Cream, 258
Flan, Black Bean, 110
Flan(s) (sweet)
  Almond, Country-Baked, 245
  Coconut-Rum, 244
  Traditional, 242
Flank Steak with Port Wine
    Marinade, 134
Flounder, *in* Seafood Stew, 202
Fluke, *in* Seafood Stew, 202
Fresh Coconut and Banana Cream
    Pie, 254
Fresh Corn and Red Pepper
    Tamales, 84
Fried Pork and Onion Patties, 153
Fried Shrimp with Coconut-Beer
    Batter and Orange Cock-
    tail Sauce, 42
Fried Sweet Plantains, 75
Fried Yuca Dough with Almond
    Syrup, 252
Fritters
  Calabaza, 79
  Conch, with Cilantro Dipping
      Sauce, 44

Frozen Banana Custard, 259
Frozen Rum Mousse, 247
Fruit(s)
    Salad with Lemon-Lime Dress-
        ing, 46
    see also names of fruits

Galician Potage, 61
Game Hens, Roasted, with Bitter
        Orange Glaze, 176
Garlic
    Bitter Orange and, Pork Tender-
        loin Sautéed with, 142
    in Breast of Chicken al Ajillo, 66
    Cream of, Soup, with Cilantro, 59
    -Marinated Roasted Chicken, 181
    -Onion Dinner Muffins, 234
    Pork, Grilled, 154
    to prepare, 23
    Sauce, Yuca with, 78
    -Tomato Soup, 60
    Wine Sauce, Shrimp in, 33
Glaze(s)
    Bitter Orange, Roasted Game
        Hens with, 176
    Papaya, Roasted Chicken with, 174
Golden Baked Chicken with
        Tomatoes, Olives and Capers,
        178
Gravy, Creamy, Hot Pepper Pork
        Chops with, 156
Green chilies. *See* Chilies
Green peppers. *See* Peppers
Grilled Garlic Pork, 154
Grouper
    for dolphin *in* Broiled Dolphin
        with Sweet Red Pepper
        and Papaya Chutney, 198
    Pan-Fried, with Almonds, 191
    for pompano *in* Poached Pompano
        with Orange-Rum Sauce, 210
Guava
    Batido, 275
    Ice Cream, 263
    notes on, 23
    puree, notes on, 263, 274

Haddock, salt, for cod *in* Salt Cod,
        Island Style, 192

Halibut, *in* Seafood Stew, 202
Ham
    in Chicken and Rice Stew, 164
    Cider-and-Mango-Roasted, 145
    hock
        in Red Bean Soup, 67
        in Traditional Black Bean
            Soup, 56
        in White Bean and Tomato
            Soup, 64
    in Paella, 302
    in Pasteles, 132
    and Potato Croquettes, Spicy, 148
    in Rolled Stuffed Steak, 135
Homemade Spanish Sausage, 144
Honey-Rum-Baked Black Beans, 108
Hot Chocolate Coffee, 272
Hot Pepper Pork Chops with
        Creamy Gravy, 156
Hot Rum Toddy, 295

Ice cream(s)
    Coconut, 260
    Frozen Banana Custard, 259
    Guava, 263
    makers, notes on, 239
    Mango, 261
    Pineapple, 262
    Vanilla Bean, 257
Iced Cuban Coffee, 271

Land crabs, notes on, 202
Langosta
    in Lobster and Red Peppers in a
        Rice Mold, 197
    notes on, 197
Lemon-Lime Dressing, Fruit Salad
        with, 46
Lentil(s)
    notes on, 18
    and Rice, Vegetable Soup with, 70
    Salad, Chilled, with Spicy Vinai-
        grette, 107
Lime
    Daiquiri, 287
    Lemon-, Dressing, Fruit Salad
        with, 46

Lobster
    and Red Peppers in a Rice Mold,
        197
    rock, tail, *in* Paella, 308
    in Seafood Stew, 202
    spiny. *See* Langosta
Long-Grain White Rice, 95

Malanga
    in Ajiaco, 83
    notes on, 23
Mango(s)
    Butter, 235
    Cider-and-, -Roasted Ham, 145
    to cut, 24
    Daiquiri, 288
    in Fruit Salad with Lemon-Lime
        Dressing, 46
    Ice Cream, 261
    notes on, 23
    Papaya-, Batido, 276
    Sauce, Flaming, over Homemade
        Vanilla Ice Cream, 258
Marinade, Port Wine, Flank Steak
        with, 134
Marinated Black Bean Salad, 102
Marinated Conch Salad, 201
Mashed Green Plantains, 76
Mayonnaise, 41
Meat
    Filling, Sweet and Spicy, Tamale
        Pie with, 127
    -and-Onion-Stuffed Turnovers, 130
    see also Beef; Pork
Menu, for Cuban feast, 301
Milk
    Coconut, 278
    Cuban Coffee with, 270
    Punch, 297
Milkshakes, fruit. *See* Batidos
Mojito, 282
Mold(s)
    Rice, Lobster and Red Peppers in
        a, 197
    of Yellow Rice with Shrimp,
        Scallops, and Red Pepper, 112
Mousse, Rum, Frozen, 247

Muffins
    Coconut, 232
    Dinner, Garlic-Onion, 234
    Red Pepper, Spicy, 233

Oil, Achiote, 120
Old-Fashioned Cornmeal Pudding,
        250
Olives, Tomatoes, and Capers,
        Crispy Baked Chicken
        with, 178
Omelet, Vegetable and Cheese, 88
Onion(s)
    Cilantro, Tomato, and Snapper
        Grilled in Foil with, 209
    Garlic-, Dinner Muffins, 234
    Meat-and-, -Stuffed Turnovers, 130
    to peel, slice, and chop, 24
    and Peppers, Sautéed, Chicken
        Croquettes with, 172
    Pork and, Patties, Fried, 153
    Sweet, Roasted, 305
    Tomatoes, and Peppers, Spicy
        Black Beans with, 103
Orange(s)
    bitter
        and Garlic, Pork Tenderloin
            Sautéed with, 142
        Glaze, Roasted Game Hens
            with, 176
        juice, *in* Crispy Fried Mari-
            nated Chicken, 180
        juice, notes on, 18
        juice, *in* Roast Suckling Pig, 302
        notes on, 18, 176
    Bread, 227
    Cocktail Sauce, Coconut-Beer Batter
        and, Fried Shrimp with, 42
    -Raisin Cornmeal Stuffing, 306
    -Rum Sauce, Poached Pompano
        with, 210
Oxtail Stew, 122

Paella, 308
Palomilla Steak, 123
Pan-Fried Grouper with Almonds,
        191

Papaya(s)
-Banana Batido, 274
Braised Loin of Pork with, 141
Chutney, 41
Spicy Crab Cakes with, 40
in Fruit Salad with Lemon-Lime
Dressing, 46
Glaze, Roasted Chicken with, 174
-Mango Batido, 276
for mango *in* Mango Butter, 235
notes on, 24
Pork, Sweet and Sour, 157
and Raisin Bread, 224
Sauce, Spicy, Baby Back Ribs
with, 143
Sweet Red Pepper and, Chutney,
Broiled Dolphin with, 198
Vegetables and, Spicy Chicken
Sauté with, 167
Pastel de Maíz, 182
Pasteles, 132
Peach Daiquiri, 289
Peas, Yellow Rice and, 100
Pepper
black, notes on, 25
cayenne, notes on, 25
Hot, Pork Chops with Creamy
Gravy, 156
Peppers
green
in Peppers Stuffed with Spanish
Sausage and Tomato, 86
in Spicy Stuffed Peppers with
Tomato Sauce, 128
notes on, 25
Onions and, Sautéed, Chicken
Croquettes with, 172
red
Fresh Corn and, Tamales, 84
Lobster and, in a Rice Mold, 197
Muffins, Spicy, 233
Shrimp, Scallops, and, Mold of
Yellow Rice with, 112
Sweet, and Papaya Chutney,
Broiled Dolphin with, 198
Sweet, Sauce, Tuna Steak with,
195

Peppers (*cont'd*)
to roast, 25
Stuffed
with Spanish Sausage, Rice,
and Tomato, 86
Spicy, with Tomato Sauce, 128
Tomatoes, Onions, and, Spicy
Black Beans with, 103
Picadillo, 121
Pie(s)
Cream, Fresh Coconut and Ba-
nana, 254
Tamale, with Sweet and Spicy
Meat Filling, 127
Pig, Suckling, Roast, 302
Pimiento
Salsa, Sausage Empanadas with, 34
Tomato-, Bread, 220
Piña Colada, 292
Pineapple
Daiquiri, 290
in Fruit Salad with Lemon-Lime
Dressing, 46
Ice Cream, 262
Plantain(s)
in Ajiaco, 83
Bread, Sweet, 224
Butter-Rum, Sautéed, 307
Croquettes with Tomato-Cilantro
Vinaigrette, 36
Custard, 246
green
Mashed, 76
to peel, 26
notes on, 25, 73
Soup, Sweet, 55
Sweet, Fried, 75
in Sweet and Spicy Calabaza
Soup, 68
in Tostones, 77
Planter's Punch, 296
Poached Pompano with Orange-
Rum Sauce, 210
Pollock, salt, for cod *in* Salt Cod,
Island Style, 192
Pompano
Poached, with Orange-Rum Sauce,
210

Pompano *(cont'd)*
  with Shrimp Sauce, 207
Pork
  Baby Back Ribs with Spicy
    Papaya Sauce, 143
  chops
    Cornmeal-and-Raisin-Stuffed,
      155
    Hot Pepper, with Creamy
      Gravy, 156
    in Sweet and Sour Papaya
      Pork, 157
    in Wine Sauce, 152
  doneness of, to check, 139
  Garlic, Grilled, 154
  Loin of
    with Papaya, Braised, 141
    Roast, Cuban-Chinese, 158
  and Onion Patties, Fried, 153
  Papaya, Sweet and Sour, 157
  in Pasteles, 132
  Roast, with Peppered Black Bean
    Sauce, 146
  side. *See* Side pork
  Suckling Pig, Roast, 302
  Tamales, 150
  Tenderloin Sautéed with Bitter
    Orange and Garlic, 142
  White Beans and, Sweet Baked, 105
  see also Sausage
Port Wine Marinade, Flank Steak
  with, 134
Potage, Galician, 61
Potato(es)
  Ham and, Croquettes, Spicy, 148
  Shrimp, Corn, and, Soup, 63
  see also Boniatos
Pot Roast, Cuban, 126
Presidente, 281
Pudding(s)
  Cornmeal, Old-Fashioned, 250
  Diplomatic, 241
  Rice
    Classic, 249
    Rum, 310
  Rum-Raisin, Baked, 248
  see also Flans (sweet)

Punch(es)
  Calypso, Spiced, 277
  Milk, 297
  Planter's, 296
  Rum, 296
  Sangría, 297

Raisin(s)
  Almond-, Bread, 226
  Cornmeal-and-, -Stuffed Pork
    Chops, 155
  Orange-, Cornmeal Stuffing,
    306
  Papaya and, Bread, 225
  Rum-, Pudding, Baked, 248
Red beans. *See* Beans
Red peppers. *See* Peppers
Rice
  Black Beans and, 98
    Rum-Flavored, 101
  chicken and. *See* Chicken
  Lentils, and, Vegetable Soup
    with, 70
  Mold, Lobster and Red Peppers
    in a, 197
  notes on, 26
  puddings. *See* Puddings
  Red Beans and, 104
  in Spicy Stuffed Peppers with
    Tomato Sauce, 128
  Valencia
    notes on, 26
    in Paella, 308
  White, Long-Grain, 95
  Yellow, 99
    Mold of, with Shrimp, Scallops,
      and Red Pepper, 112
    and Peas, 100
Roasted Boniatos, 304
Roasted Chicken with Papaya
  Glaze, 174
Roasted Game Hens with Bitter
  Orange Glaze, 176
Roasted Sweet Onions, 305
Roast Pork with Peppered Black
  Bean Sauce, 146
Roast Suckling Pig, 302

Rock lobster tail, *in* Paella, 308
Rolled Stuffed Steak, 135
Rolls, Cassava, 222
Ropa Vieja, 119
Rum
  Butter-, Plantains, Sautéed, 307
  Cocktail, 283
  Coconut-, Flan, 244
  and Coconut Water, 293
  in Cuba Libre, 280
  in Cuban Cocktail, 284
  in Cuban Special, 285
  -Flavored Black Beans and Rice,
    101
  -Glazed Boniatos, 82
  Honey-, -Baked Black Beans, 108
  in Mojito, 282
  Mousse, Frozen, 247
  Orange-, Sauce, Poached Pom-
    pano with, 210
  in Piña Colada, 292
  in Planter's Punch, 296
  in Presidente, 281
  Punch, 296
  -Raisin Pudding, Baked, 248
  Rice Pudding, 310
  Shrimp, Sweet, 38
  -Spiked Coffee, 273
  Sponge Cakes with, 256
  Swizzle, 286
    Super, 286
  Toddy
    Cold, 294
    Hot, 295
  in Yellow Bird, 292
  see also Daiquiri

Saffron Sauce, Snapper with,
    206
Salad(s)
  Bean, Tri-Colored, with Bacon
    Dressing, 106
  Fruit, with Lemon-Lime Dress-
    ing, 46
  Lentil, Chilled, with Spicy Vinai-
    grette, 107
  Marinated Conch, 201

Salad(s) (*cont'd*)
  Pimiento, Sausage Empanadas
    with, 34
  Tomato-Caper, Breaded Shrimp
    with, 204
Salt cod. *See* Cod
Salt haddock, for cod *in* Salt Cod,
    Island Style, 192
Salt pollock, for cod *in* Salt Cod,
    Island Style, 192
Sangría, 297
Sauce(s)
  Black Bean, Shrimp with, 211
  Cocktail, Orange, Coconut-Beer
    Batter, Fried Shrimp with, 42
  Coconut, Snapper in, 196
  Cream, Light, Coconut-Stuffed
    Chicken Breasts with, 168
  Dipping, Cilantro, Conch Fritters
    with, 44
  Garlic
    Yuca with, 78
  Orange-Rum, Poached Pompano
    with, 210
  Papaya, Spicy, Baby Back Ribs
    with, 143
  Saffron, Snapper with, 206
  Shrimp, Pompano with, 207
  sofrito. *See* Sofrito
  Sweet Red Pepper, Tuna Steak
    with, 195
  Tomato, Spicy Stuffed Peppers
    with, 128
  Wine
    Garlic, Shrimp in, 33
    Pork Chops in, 152
  see also Dressings; Salsas
Sausage(s)
  Empanadas with Pimiento Salsa,
    34
  smoked, *in* Black Bean Chili, 111
  Spanish
    Homemade, 144
    and Tomato, Peppers Stuffed
      with, 86
  see also Chorizo
Sautéed Butter-Rum Plantains, 307

Scallops, Shrimp, and Red Pepper,
    Mold of Yellow Rice with, 112
Scrod, *in* Escabeche, 39
Seafood
  Stew, 202
  see also names of fish and shellfish
Shrimp
  with Black Bean Sauce, 211
  Breaded, with Tomato-Caper
    Salsa, 204
  Corn, and Potato Soup, 63
  Creole, 200
  Fried, with Coconut-Beer Batter
    and Orange Cocktail Sauce, 42
  in Garlic Wine Sauce, 33
  notes on, 26
  in Paella, 308
  Sauce, Pompano with, 207
  Scallops, and Red Pepper, Mold
    of Yellow Rice with, 112
  in Seafood Stew, 202
  Sweet Rum, 38
Side pork
  in Conch Chowder, 65
  notes on, 27, 65
  in Sweet Baked White Beans and
    Pork, 105
Snapper
  Black-Bean-Steamed, 194
  in Coconut Sauce, 196
  in Escabeche, 39
  Grilled in Foil with Cilantro,
    Tomato, and Onion, 209
  with Saffron Sauce, 206
Sofrito
  Grilled Chicken, 184
  notes on, 195
  Sauce, 185
Sole, *in* Seafood Stew, 202
Soup(s)
  Black Bean, Traditional, 56
  Calabaza, Sweet and Spicy, 68
  Chicken and Rice, 66
  Conch Chowder, 65
  Cucumber and Avocado, Cold, 62
  Garlic
    Cream of, with Cilantro, 59

Soup(s) (*cont'd*)
  -Tomato, 60
  Plantain, Sweet, 55
  Red Bean, 67
  Shrimp, Corn, and Potato, 63
  Vegetable, with Lentils and Rice, 70
  White Bean and Tomato, 64
  Yuca, Chilled, 58
  see also Stocks
Spanish sausage. *See* Sausage; Chorizo
Spiced Calypso Punch, 277
Spicy Black Beans with Tomatoes,
    Onions, and Peppers, 103
Spicy Chicken Sauté with Vegeta-
    bles and Papaya, 167
Spicy Cornbread with Green
    Chilies, 228
Spicy Crab Cakes with Papaya
    Chutney, 40
Spicy Grilled Tuna, 208
Spicy Ham and Potato Croquettes,
    148
Spicy Red Pepper Muffins, 233
Spicy Stuffed Peppers with Tomato
    Sauce, 128
Sponge Cakes with Rum, 256
Steak(s)
  Tuna, with Sweet Red Pepper
    Sauce, 195
  see also Beef
Stew(s)
  Chicken and Rice, 164
  Seafood, 202
Stock(s)
  Beef, 54
  Chicken, 52
  Fish, 51
Strawberries, *in* Fruit Salad with
    Lemon-Lime Dressing, 46
String beans, *in* Tri-Colored Salad
    with Bacon Dressing, 106
Stuffing, Cornmeal, Orange-Raisin,
    306
Suckling Pig, Roast, 302
Super Rum Swizzle, 286
Sweet Baked White Beans and
    Pork, 105

Sweet Plantain Bread, 224
Sweet Plantain Soup, 55
Sweet Rum Shrimp, 38
Sweet and Sour Papaya Pork, 157
Sweet and Spicy Calabaza Soup, 68
Sweet and Spicy Cilantro Chicken, 177
Swordfish, *in* Escabeche, 39
Syrup, Almond, Fried Yuca Dough with, 252

Tamale(s)
  Fresh Corn and Red Pepper, 84
  Pie with Sweet and Spicy Meat Filling, 127
  Pork, 150
Tilefish, *in* Escabeche, 39
Toddy. *See* Rum
Tomato(es)
  -Caper Salsa, Breaded Shrimp with, 204
  Cilantro
    and Onion, Snapper Grilled in Foil with, 209
    Vinaigrette, Plantain Croquettes with, 36
  Garlic-, Soup, 60
  Olives, and Capers, Crispy Baked Chicken with, 178
  Onions, and Peppers, Spicy Black Beans with, 103
  to peel, 27
  Sauce, Spicy Stuffed Peppers with, 128
  Spanish Sausage and, Peppers Stuffed with, 86
  White Bean and, Soup, 64
Tostones, 77
Traditional Black Bean Soup, 56
Traditional Flan, 242
Tri-Colored Bean Salad with Bacon Dressing, 106
Tuna
  Grilled, Spicy, 208

Tuna (*cont'd*)
  Steak with Sweet Red Pepper Sauce, 195
  Turnovers, Meat-and-Onion-Stuffed, 130

Valencia rice. *See* Rice
Vanilla
  Ice Cream, Homemade, Flaming Mango Sauce over, 258
  Bean Ice Cream, 257
Vegetable(s)
  and Cheese Omelet, 88
  and Papaya, Spicy Chicken Sauté, 167
  Soup with Lentils and Rice, 70
  see also names of vegetables
Vinaigrette(s)
  Avocados with, 90
  Spicy, Chilled Lentil Salad with, 107
  Tomato-Cilantro, Plantain Croquettes with, 36

Water, coconut. *See* Coconut
White beans. *See* Beans
White kidney beans. *See* Beans
White Rice, Long-Grain, 95
Wine
  Port, Marinade, Flank Steak with, 134
  sauces. *See* Sauces

Yellow rice. *See* Rice
Yellow Bird, 292
Yuca
  in Ajiaco, 83
  to cook and mash, 28
  Dough, Fried, with Almond Syrup, 252
  with Garlic Sauce, 78
  notes on, 27, 73
  to peel, 27
  Soup, Chilled, 58
  Stuffed with Shredded Beef, Baked, 124
  see also Cassava

ABOUT LINETTE CREEN

Linette Creen is a professional cookbook writer, cooking teacher, and caterer. She has had a lifelong interest in Cuban cuisine, and in her teenage years in Miami began learning how to prepare authentic Cuban foods by cooking with experienced home cooks in the Cuban-American community.

In the early 1980s, Linette ran a family-owned retail and wholesale seafood store and catering business in Alaska, where she collected her recipes into *The Great Alaskan Seafood Cookbook* (Grundman Marketing, 1983). This book was later adapted and expanded into *The Jewel Lake Seafood Market Cookbook*, which was published by Simon and Schuster in 1988 (under her maiden name, Hoglund).

After returning to New York City, Linette Creen spent three years as the youngest female member of the New York Stock Exchange. She left the financial world to continue her cooking career.

In recent years, she returned to Miami, where chefs were using the traditional Cuban ingredients in creative new ways, and the recipes they taught her are included in this book, along with the classic Cuban dishes.

Recently married, she now lives in Cold Spring Harbor, New York, where she caters parties and other special events. She also teaches cooking courses at the Huntington School District's Adult Continuing Education Program. She has studied at the French Culinary Institute.